In Light, Love and Communion

Memoirs of a Psychic Healer

In Light, Love and Communion

Memoirs of a Psychic Healer

Dr Ramakant K Keni

AUTHORSPRESS

Worldwide Circulation through Authorspress Global Network
First Published 2009
by
Authorspress
E-35/103, Jawahar Park
Laxmi Nagar, Delhi-110 092
e-mail: authorspress@yahoo.com

In Light, Love and Communion: Memoirs of a Psychic Healer
ISBN 978-81-7273-478-7

Printed in India at Tarun Offset, Delhi.

This book is
dedicated to
the One and Only
Divine ***SAI BABA***
of Shirdi

Preface

I must begin with a few words from William S. Baring-Gould's introduction to the definitive edition of Sherlock Homes stories and novels: "If you have not read a Sherlock Holmes story... advance immediately to the opening story.... Then, if you have a mind to, kindly return to this introduction." I echo the great Sherlockian: if you have not read Dr. Ramakant Keni's books, *please* ignore this preface and proceed immediately to the first page of this book. *And*, you *need not* return to this preface.

*****

At that time we (my wife, our two sons—the older 14 and the younger 6—and me) were residing at Puri-on-Sea, the sacred abode of Lord Jagannath, where my wife and I were teaching at the SCS College. I was suffering from what my physicians had diagnosed as ones which defied total cure; both were related to the mind. Both the "diseases" (I have kept the word, *disease*, within quotation marks, for as Dr. Keni—today I address him as "Papa"—was to assure me again and again over the next several years, that I did *not* have any *disease*, that it was something vastly different from what I had been thinking it be). I must confess however that I was going through two different modes of unbearably terrible pain: while one was purely physical but as old as forty years, the other was both mental and physical, but relatively shorter—a little over three years.

It was in the summer of 1993 that my wife's younger brother—a banker—asked me, rather hesitantly, if I was willing to be treated by Dr.Ramakant Keni, the Head of the Parapsychology Cell at Bombay Hospital, Mumbai, and one of the country's most respected psychic healers. He said that a close friend of his—a brilliant student and then a successful engineer with a large public limited organisation—used to suffer from the ailment that was somewhat similar to the second and younger of my two problems and had been totally cured by Dr. Keni at a time when he was on the verge of losing his job. My brother-in-law's words were reassuring, for I had already met his friend, who was now as light and happy as a bird in flight. I could not believe that he once was suffering from anything at all. I was further asked if I might like to visit Dr. Keni in his chamber at the Bombay Hospital.

I have been—and perhaps will continue to be—a very bad traveller, so the possibility of a visit to Mumbai was slim and remote, although my wife, my brother-in-law and his friend were eager to accompany me to Mumbai. The young engineer told about Dr. Keni's "distant healing." I was willing to write to Dr. Keni, describing my problems and enclosing one of my recent photographs. And I *did.* A week or so later I received a six-page letter from Dr. Keni, addressing me (as if he knew me over a long stretch of time) to my disbelief as "My very dear Bibhu" and then affectionately moving on to explain everything I was going through in a beautiful way in a beautiful long hand (much later I learnt that he never used a typewriter while writing letters to friends and patients)—which was as attractive and deep in its appeal to the eye and soul as each of his numerous paintings.

Our relationship in due time flowered into a friendship that is rare to find in this money-stuck world. He would then give me "distant healing," writing me letter after letter despite my long silences: apart from being a bad traveller, I am an inexcusably lazy letter-writer too! However, in a predetermined fashion, we did meet him, as they say, "by the way," while we were vacationing in Mumbai on an overdue invitation of an intimate friend working as a top officer in the Indian Customs and Excise Service. My first glimpse of Dr. Ramakant K. Keni held something fascinating and strange. His coarse-silk coat was not enough to hide a translucent body through which I could almost see the magnificently carved out statue of the Sai Baba of Shirdi. The room was filled with a slightly smoky fragrance of something that seemed to issue out of nowhere. I felt humbled by the entire atmosphere. Dr. Keni requested me to sit on a high, cushioned stool while he sat on another. He gently held my thumb for a half-minute, felt my spinal cord, placed his hand on my head for a minute. The "younger" problem quietly disappeared. He never "treated" my older problem, assuring me that it was not a problem at all and hence did not require any "healing."

When we returned home, I started receiving his published books, all of which had gone out of circulation and each of which was indeed a great gift. Several years later I received a letter in which there was a request: "Bibhu, I am a healer, not a writer. I know there are all kinds of errors in the books, except of course factual ones. I wonder if you have the time and patience to go through my books, choose two and convert them into a single book...." I clearly recall my two-line, hasty but prompt, reply: "Please don't request me further, Papa; order me to do whatever little I could do for you. I owe you a lot. . . ." My tardy, deferring nature has taken me more than twelve long years to do (I am not sure if I have done justice to the manuscript I prepared a year ago) what he requested me to. But I feel elated about the fact that it has found its place. I am grateful to Dr. Ramakant Keni for offering me a chance to "edit(!)" and coalesce his two books into one; I am indebted to my own present publishers, Authorspress, and its Managing Director and my "cosmic brother," Sudarshan Kcherry (who, like "Papa," is a firm and spontaneous devotee of Sai Baba of Shirdi and has himself written two excellent books on "The Sole Spirit"), for offering a straight 'Yes' to publishing the book you are now holding.

May the book reach its right readers.

Dhenkanal, Orissa/January 31, 2009 **_Bibhu Padhi_**

Contents

SECTION TWO

SECTION ONE

1

Introduction

A large part of the book may read like an autobiography. If it reads like one, I offer my apologies, for I feel that I am too humble a man to write an autobiography, which I think is the privilege of the famous and the great. However, my Guide, who has inspired me to write about these personal experiences, is a great soul and, as a result, an autobiographical approach cannot be altogether avoided.

You will agree with me that to be curious about different fields of knowledge is a typically human trait; so that, when we observe a Psychic Healing, through which a painful and protracted disease disappears or observe a growth being dispersed or stiff joints being loosened—in short, whenever we see incurable maladies being healed, it is but natural that we would like to know how these healings are accomplished. Often, of course, curiosity is found in combination with scepticism and doubt and a miracle healing is ascribed to either a coincidence or a delayed benefit of some medical therapy administered several years ago!

Harry Edwards of the Spiritual Healing Sanctuary, Guildford (in Surrey) in England, once said: "There must be a reason for all things and any state of change can only come from the all things and any state of change can only come from the applications of law-governed forces. But in considering how healings take place, we are faced with a fundamental difficulty. This difficulty is that we can only understand that which is within our scope. For example, it is quite impossible to give a person who has been blind from birth any description of a colour that he can understand."

The same is true of Psychic Healing, Faith or Spiritual Healing, or Contact Healing. Since, in these instances, healing comes from the non-material dimensions of the Spirit, it is impossible for us to visualise how it works, because it works through something that is not physical. The full understanding of how healing takes place is not available to us. Nevertheless, Harry Edwards, who was inspired to open his Sanctuary after a visit to India that helped develop his healing touch, has arrived at some valid conclusions. He says: "It is plain that every healing is a planned act and therefore it needs some kind of intelligence to carry it out. No one can make a rabbit-hutch unless he has a plan for it in his mind, and the necessary things to make it with. We know that this intelligence is not human because we see the healing of the incurable when all human knowledge can do no more. So this directing intelligence is superior to that of man. Since it is no human, it can only come from the Divine or the Spirit."

There are inevitable laws that govern all things in the universe. Indeed, not even a leaf can drop from a tree without the sanction of Divine Laws. It cannot, therefore, be suggested that God overrides everything. His laws of creation are quietly established through a favoured dispensation to some.

If one's hand is cut off, can we expect God to replace it with another? We would not make such a demand simply because we know what are the things that are against the established laws of creation. Hence, it can be safely conceded that Psychic Healing can take place only in accordance with the laws that govern the process of evolution and that the spirit-mediums possess the wisdom of knowing how to direct forces within this disciplined order to bring about a physical chance for the better.

Spiritual healers are familiar with two extreme types of patients: (1) those whose emotional credulity leads them to expect quick results and miracles; and (2) those who have become cynical by years of intense suffering despite modern medical therapy. The latter go in for spiritual healing as a *last* resort and that too with a negative thought that this new mode of treatment too may be doomed to failure. Both the above-mentioned mental approaches to spiritual healing are symptoms of mental disequilibrium. Healthy and positive thoughts on the contrary have the power to impart a sense of mental and spiritual upliftment. That psychic or spiritual healing is a Divine gift cannot be disputed. Often, healing takes place instantly because of a thought transmission to the realm of the spirit. It is the firm conviction of spiritualists that the strictly law-governed curative rays are produced in an appropriate and optimum quality and quantity by a discarnate Spirit possessed of superior knowledge, power and skill compared to in ordinary mortals.

Healing therefore is a scientific therapy and as such forms an integral part of the process of evolution can a person qualifying part of the process of evolution; and a person qualified in this Divine science is also a part of this plan of majestic splendour. Erik Palmtierna, author of *Horizons of Immortality*, has commented lucidly and succintly on this subject: "I am watching events, eagerly desirous, not only to guide by the whispering inner voices to our souls, but also by talking openly and directly in order to bring about a definite turn of the tide on earth and to make man realise the true purport of life and his own part in the evolution towards the ultimate source of Love and Light."

There are spiritual currents permeating the universe to which we need only to be attuned to in order to gain physical and spiritual sustenance. But though the sun gives heat, one must step out of the shadow to experience it. Though the forces of the Spirit fill the universe—and man is inherently a spiritual entity—a sincere effort toward seeking attunement is still absolutely necessary; for, it is this link which establishes the "rapport".

I am very optimistic about the future of psychic healing in India. The Bombay Hospital, a highly prestigious and research-oriented institution, is perhaps the only hospital that has allowed me to practise healing in addition to my geriatric practice. It was a bold step taken by Shri Shriyan Prasad Jain, the Chairman of the Hospital Trust. Shri Jain was perhaps guided by the Divine to do this and those who have been cured, bless him. He deserves all the credit for the courage of his firm illusion-free convictions.

Psychic healers are already permitted to visit patients in hundreds of hospitals in Britain, U.S.A, Africa, Brazil, Mexico, and several other western countries. A similar recognition in India will enable and embolden many of our cautious healers to come out in the open and offer merciful relief to many sufferers. Indian universities should shed their prejudices and recognise the value of spiritual or divine healing. It is indeed an irony that though spiritual healing is a part of India's rich heritage, today, India has forgotten this priceless tradition, while Western countries are forging ahead in employing and tapping this great gift inherent in man.

2

A Divinely Ordained Plan

It was in the beginning of 1971 that I was privileged to meet a highly educated and vibrant personality who was eighty years of age then, but quite healthy despite his age.

It was he who first introduced initiated me into spiritualism and psychic phenomena. He came into my life as if the meeting were a divinely ordained plan. This was evident from the fact that he persisted in my taking up psychic healing as a career. I held out for a long time because my field was strictly medical and I could not get reconciled to the idea of settling down as a healer. In later years, however, I realised that medical science and psychic healing are synonymous. This fact is corroborated by the experiences of great healers, which have been published with authentic data. Unfortunately, I have been dissuaded from using the name of my elderly guide. For my readers' convenience, I have therefore taken the liberty of calling this person "Mr. Krishnan", which is the most suitable name for one who had surrendered to Lord Krishna as his "*Ishta Devata.*"

One day, Mr. Krishnan took me round his library in which he has apparently invested a large fortune. He took out for me two books which he wanted me to go through seriously. The books were by Harry Edwards and Maurice Barbanell—both very important persons connected with psychic healing and spiritualism for several decades. Though I read these books conscientiously, I still felt sceptical about the efficacy of such modes of healing. I frankly expressed my feelings to Mr. Krishnan who, however, was not daunted and persisted in trying to convert me by giving me more and more books until I myself was convinced that spiritualism was not only a great asset in life, but also a great mission of one's life-work. All my erstwhile atheistic tendencies disappeared and I began to feel a genuine faith in the existence of God, particularly when I could see with my own eyes the materialisation of objects and when I actually had experiences of communication with the other world. When I found that Spirits do exist and "contact" can be established with them through reliable mediums, all my doubts vanished and I was filled with piety.

The amazing universe and its immaculate working convinced me of the existence of higher unseen powers. To those who still have doubts spiritualism and God's healing intentions, I would like to mention an important paragraph published in the *Time* magazine, December 26, 1977, according to which an increasing number of scientists now agree with the statement of astronomer Robert Jastrow, founder and Director of NASA's Goddard Institute: "Since it is impossible to prove whether life on earth was created by the will of some supreme creative Being or evolved spontaneously, the choice either way is an act of faith. Even among highly secular folk there is a general disposition to assume, as never before, that if God does not exist, it may be necessary for man to invent Him."

It was only after studying in depth the books of well-known authors on this subject, that I decided to go in for a test, which would reveal whether I had in me the ability of healing spiritually. The test was a simple one. I bought identical bouquets of flowers and kept them in two vases filled with water from the same jug. The vases were placed side by side on the same table so that climatic conditions would be the same for both. I "healed" the flowers of one vase only, and put a tag on that vase: "Healed flowers". I was happy and surprised to find that the "healed" bunch of flowers outlived the other by six days! This could not be a coincidence by any stretch of imagination or the usual botanical explanations. This experiment induced in me a lot of faith in "healing" and also convinced me of my own potentiality as a healer.

In 1972, I had acute pain in my back which confined me to the bed. The X-rays indicated lumbar and cervical spondylitis. My fast deteriorating condition compelled me to consult both an orthopaedic surgeon as well as a neurophysician. While the former prescribed about 20 tablets a day, plus diathermy, corset and traction, the latter threatened me with a verdict of a possible paralysis if I did not take complete bed-rest. I was therefore in bed and felt thoroughly miserable—not only physically but mentally too with the thought that I would soon be an invalid for my rest of my life. During this plight Mr. Krishnan again came to my help. He asked me to write to Harry Edwards, requesting him to give me "absent" healing—not only for the physical disease, but also for my mental agony. I did this immediately and in less than a week I received an urgent message from Harry Edwards, reassuring me that "absent" healing had been started and that I would soon feel better. In fact, I started feeling better no sooner than I had posted my letter to Harry. This was not just a mental illusion because indeed I was suddenly relieved of my acute pain. A week later I could go about my work without the corset or any medication. Since then my back has never given me any trouble despite extensive travelling, work and worries.

This is a true record of a miracle cure I received from a healer from a distance of miles. My respect and admiration for Harry Edwards gathered up tremendously. Harry Edwards has a similar case history published in 1966 with the name and address of the patient he treated. I am reproducing it here: "A lady had been suffering from a curvature of the spine. She had become a hunchback. The X-ray photographs showed the gross wedging of the vertebrae. Pressure on the nerves that emerge from between the vertebrae numbed them and her legs became partially paralysed. She could only hobble along with the aid of two sticks. She suffered from agonising pains continuously. She was just forty years old and had been under the care of hospitals and other specialists for many years. Could she ever be made upright again, walking easily and normally? The medical verdict would be 'impossible' and yet after one visit to our Sanctuary, this transformation took place. Her spine was re-aligned, all symptoms of paralysis and pain left her. She was able to walk normally without the aid of sticks. Today this same lady has become a farmer's wife and is even able to drive a tractor. In gratitude she has even opened a healing centre."

But though spiritual healing was confirmed as a known or felt-reality, I myself had not yet started healing and I had no proof of my own healing powers. However, six months later, when I went to visit Mr. Krishnan at his residence, I was told that he was attending a "séance". Mr. Krishnan, on hearing about my visit to his house, sent a message inviting me to the séance meeting. I know too well today that this too was well-planned: I knew that I was actually led to the séance by unseen forces. This was my first experience of witnessing a séance and a powerful medium functioning in a kind of semi-trance. People were seated around on chairs and this medium went around, stopping in front of some persons, only to pass on the "messages" from the other world of their near and dear ones who had passed away. Sometimes the medium gave inspired advice received from her own Spirit-Guide to a few chosen ones.

Though the room was filled with darkness, the medium unhesitatingly went to the right persons who were fortunate enough to receive messages from the world beyond. Of course, all were not equally privileged enough to receive these "messages". You can therefore imagine my delight and surprise when the same medium whom I had never met before, suddenly came straight up to me to tell me that she had to deliver a very important message to me from my Spirit-Guide who wanted to select me as his instrument for healing others. The medium repeated this message several times with a stern advice that I should completely free my mind of all doubts, suspicions and negative thinking. "You are the chosen one," said the medium, repeatedly.

After the meeting I had a strange, out-of-the-world feeling of being suddenly charged with a fantastic, indescribable energy. I felt I could run for miles and miles, that I had grown strong and supple wings. I had an exhilarating fever of joy and confidence. I felt that I could merely *touch* a sick person and raise him from his bed of suffering and enable him to walk. My palms had become warm and there were trembling vibrations on the tips of all my fingers. I could see lights and flames deep inside my forehead when I closed my eyes. It was as if I had been given a supreme energy, making me feel years younger than I actually was. The experience thoroughly convinced me that I could heal people through psychic energy so lovingly bestowed on me by my Spirit-Guide who, as it seemed, had waited for the right time and place to contact me, giving me the power to heal a suffering humanity. However, I continued attending the "seances" as I was anxious to receive from my Spirit-Guide more and more instructions as to the specific ways and manners in which the healing energy should be used and controlled.

In fact, attending "seances" was like a finely-graded training course. However, with regard to my eagerness to know who my Spirit-Guide was, I was asked to go a certain place in Mumbai where a very powerful medium of national and international fame established contacts with the other world through automatic writings or the planchette. Meeting my Guide was one of the most thrilling experiences of my life. I could discuss with him freely and frankly about all aspects of healing and medical treatment, particularly about the diagnosis of a disease condition through the touch of the fingertips which were divinely directed to the spot where the disease was located.

My Guide, who has been a physician-cum-surgeon on our planet for some two hundred years, has built up an international reputation and still continues his medical research on the farther side. He was internationally known for his "intuitive diagnosis", and he needed an instrument to work out his principles in this field. Many amazing experiences that threw light on psychic methods of healing had taken place in my life in 1962 and 1968.

It became clear that in 1962 my Guide chose me to be his instrument, educating me in things that were unknown to me. He started sending mysterious triggers through my hands and fingers which revealed both the location and the nature of the diseases.

It was in 1968 that I was involved in an unusual and remarkable case, the significance of which was explained to me later at a séance meeting. A gentleman from the suburbs of Mumbai summoned me to see his seventy-year-old mother. I was asked to come at once as the old lady was critically ill. When I reached the place, I found the patient in a hopeless condition. An eminent physician who was there before me told me that is was a hundred-per cent fatal case, as the lady's blood pressure had fallen to 60/40. The physician wondered how the lady could live in this condition, with a totally dysfunctional bladder for more than ten hours! It is difficult to believe that anyone could survive in such a condition (the case has been duly recorded with the patient's name and address). The members of the family did not wish to remove the patient to the hospital. They just waited for her to pass away. Calling me was only a part of her son's duty. Sitting beside the patient, almost automatically I opened my bag, and inexplicably, a bulb of Mephentine injection and also an ampoule of Atropine slipped out of my bag and fell on my lap, as if God were indicating that these were the appropriate drugs whereby the lady could be saved. I took the risk of giving these injections, though the other physician kept looking at me disapprovingly and with sarcasm. The blood pressure was then taken thirty minutes after the injection, and to my great relief the pressure had improved considerably. The lady also passed copious urine. She was removed to a nursing home where she was treated only with nutritional care and kept under observation. She was discharged after a fortnight and was still alive at the time of writing this book (1984) and quite active in dispensing her daily activities. The curious circumstances of her recovery were explained to me much later. Thus with this first and amazingly successful healing, I was launched on a career of a spiritual healer...and, thereafter, life became a challenge !

3

My Spiritual Guide

The way One's Guide Helps His Instrument is indeed quite interesting. More often than not, the manner of help that is received is incredible. The help that I have received is immeasurable. It is the most precious, useful and important help from famous physician-surgeon on "the other side," to a medical man—his instrument on "this side." I cannot resist quoting two instances.

A patient comes in with a number of vague-sounding complaints that baffle the doctor, and diagnosis becomes a problem. The patient is therefore put on experimental treatment and in the end he is not cured but becomes worse. I would like to tell you how in such cases, inspired and timely help has come to me on innumerable occasions. The patient who lies down on the couch is told not to say a word about his trouble. The fingers do the searching around his back where too they do not find anything abnormal. Now the fingers move around his abdomen and suddenly there is a sort of magnetic pulling force pushing the fingers towards the location of the pain.

The indication of the spot on the abdomen or the chest or the region of pelvis does not solve the problem, however, nor is it a diagnosis, but you *do* come to know the correct area of the trouble. Fingers are lifted away from the spot and fresh energy is collected to proceed further with more investigations. Now the fingers go back to the abdomen and there is a definite pull from the place under which the appendix is located. Now the diagnosis is almost complete. In the same way the pain in the chest may be vague and not diagnosable in spite of investigations, but the healer's fingers hold on correctly to the concerned limb indicating clearly the exact spot.

In spite of all these clear indications, one may not know the precise drug to be prescribed and the adequate dosage to remove the disease. The real test of the help from the Guide is when the healer writes down or rather when there is a presence of "automatic writing" under the column "Findings or Diagnosis" (on the case papers)—words like acute giardiasis or inflamed appendix or a psychosomatic syndrome. The pen is guided by the same force to write down the name of the drug and the desired dosage; not only this but also words reading "for 20 days" or "for 30 days". It is really fantastic. It is indeed incredible, but true. This is the greatest achievement in Psychic Medicine where the right type of treatment flows out from the nib and the patient is cured in as many days as he is expected to be cured, as per the prediction of the "automatic writing."

Surprisingly enough this was seen happening in my cases even five years before I met Mr. Krishnan. I have already said earlier that our meeting was planned by divine forces. I would like to illustrate one such case of "intuitive diagnosis". A young woman who was referred to me by a doctor from Pune was complaining of pain in the lower back for several years. It was so acute a pain that she was unable to squat on the floor and pray. At the same time it was not there all the time. It was therefore a confusing pain, erratic in nature, which came on and passed away intermittently. The lady went to several doctors and was treated with various drugs. Her pathology did not reveal any abnormality. Finally, she was considered a psychosomatic patient and was treated with sedative due to which she felt better. But the pain returned when she was off sedation. She came from a healing session and there was receptivity from all the parts of the body which clearly indicated that she suffered from no disease until at last my fingers were drawn towards the cervical region and the patient felt better with fresh energy and vibrations on that spot. The X-ray confirmed the mysterious, until then undiagnosed disease, as cervical spondylitis where plenty of healing energy was given every week for a period of six months and the lady was completely cured.

Healing has never produced adverse reactions of any kind. As a rule, patients are conscious of the healing presence through a feeling of upliftment and inner happiness. Thus the removal of stress leads to the removal of the cause of the trouble. Therefore, psychic healing is eminently creative and contrary to a widespread belief, it is fully rational in its results. It is the result, not of application but restoration. Its purpose is not to make anything different but to perpetuate that which is. We all know that an orange is unquestionably a good and nourishing fruit. If it were not so, there would be no purpose behind its growth. The fact that when it is plucked off the tree, it is seen to be defective does not disprove its basic nutritive condition. The orange which has gone bad is the good orange which has deteriorated. It is "ill". The fault of its disfiguring does not lie in the orange. It is to be found either in some inherent weakness or an attack from outside: it is mostly because the stem which linked the orange to the branch was weak. Consequently (and scientifically or rationally or logically), the orange falls and is damaged. Its "illness" may be traced to outside interference and infection. Whatever the cause, the effect is unnatural and can, through appropriate methods, be remedied or cured. The same is the case with human beings and their maladies. Man, like the orange or a mango, is prone to weakness within, vulnerable to attacks from without. It is therefore necessary to strengthen the link which binds the orange to the branch and similarly to unite man with his source.

Health is normality. Illness indicates the need to correct a state of abnormality. This can be done through healing—"absent healing" or "contact healing." Can an electrically operated radio-set, in spite of new wiring and the latest type of plugs be of any use or value if there is no connection with the source of electricity? It is a dead set until it is connected to the source of its "power". Such is the mystical element in spiritual or psychic healing. It reveals the mystical element in that it tries to re-establish the powerful relationship between man and his Creator.

There appears to be a dichotomy on the whole between the brands of psychic healing lately gaining popularity as mankind is evolving towards the psychic frontiers and the forces of reconstruction and goodness are ever-present and manifesting themselves in varying forms throughout history. The entire world is moving towards an overall psychic phase when communication with and understanding of the world beyond death will become relatively much easier, since men will be more and more sensitive and intelligent and better informed about spiritual subjects.

The part the healer plays is very simple. It is not the healer who is the healing director. He is only the sensitive instrument that the spirit-doctors use to act as a conveyor and a transformer of important "spirit-energies" in order to produce the desired changes in the body of the patient. That is the wonder of it. The healing cannot take place without the healer, and the healer cannot be used if he does not devote much time in establishing the gift of attunement with the Spirit. Behind all healings are the virtues of love and compassion. If the healer does not posses these, then, he would not be willing to give his time and service for those who are suffering. A healer is not supposed to make any promises. Healing results depend on the individual receptivity of a patient to the healing process. Harry Edwards explained in one of his letters to a father who lost his son in the following words: "God has given to us the laws of Creation, and the intelligence to live wisely within them, as far as we can understand them. It is within the scope of those laws that healing can and does so much—not as a gift from God, or as an act of magic—but as a spirit science. Spiritual Healing is not omnipotent—it is bounded by the laws of creation."

This is a very logical explanation where healing cannot avert the inevitable. It is primarily an act of attunement, a linking with those forces—psychic, physical and spiritual—which animate the universe. It is a standing apart from the turmoil of existence to replenish and re-orient the Spirit. It is the re-establishment of our ancient bond with nature, and through nature, with the Divine.

4

What is Healing?

Psychic or spiritual healing involves the removal of a disease and other mental-cum-physical disharmonies through an employment of spiritual forces in terms of a human instrument, known as a "Healer-Medium". Healing has more than half-a-dozen aspects, which are now acknowledged all over Europe, the Far East and many parts of Asia. They comprise contact healing and absent healing, spirit healing, colour healing and psychic surgery, on all of which there is authentic documentation. Today, sick and ailing people are being cured by this, which has given new hope to millions. The psychic healer marches from triumph to triumph and from miracle to miracle, assuring the sick that a day will soon dawn when Spiritual Healing will be *the* accepted order of healing—accepted for the natural law that it is — and not seen as a miracle or coincidence.

The world "heal" comes from root-word, *whole*, and "healing" is "making whole" in some special sense. As we know, saints have had great powers of healing, but they used these at their own discretion, as opposed to "cursing", which implies a kind of "disintegration". In conformity with "a higher will", healing is "integration" and is intimately allied to "blessing".

Through the psychic healer, there manifests a power which we believe is natural and divine, which stimulates the patient's life-force and encourages it to perform its task of recuperation. The healer is merely a channel. A psychic healer may not cure every disease or every patient he may treat. But it is a fact that *no mode of therapy, however modern and scientific, can claim total healing.* Each has its successes and its failures. *Psychic therapy however has far better cure possibilities even after other therapies have failed.* This has been proved with case histories (a few of which are cited elsewhere in this book). Most other methods relieve symptoms but tend to leave the cause untouched. Real health is achieved when there is natural harmony between body, mind and spirit, not otherwise.

We should remind ourselves that man is a spiritual being whose mind extends beyond the normal needs of this terrene world in order to produce non-physical states. The submerged or hidden parts of the mind are in touch with active spiritual beings, who play their part in the remarkable cures effected by the psychic healer. There is a difference between body and mind which is so profound that only a miracle could account for their union, and since God alone could perform miracles, it is an undeniable proof of His existence. Spiritual healers take this point of view, regarding the body merely as the instrument through which the human mind is able to experience this terrene world of cure and health.

Without a deep and inherent desire to help another to heal, no one can become a good healer. Good healers are generally known to be deeply religious at heart, deriving much of their success from a deep faith is something or the other—either in the Almighty God or in a specific deity or a departed saint. Without this faith, no healing is possible. Doubt has a negative effect so far as healing is concerned. Faith, a mysterious mental phenomenon, acts as a link. The concept of faith in the case of intelligent beings works throughout the cosmos. It removes negative thoughts and makes it congenial for the curative processes. No "Spirit Healing" takes place unless the cause for disharmony is removed. This is where spirit healing is immeasurably superior to orthodox medical treatment. After all, medical treatment is more often than not concerned with the treatment of the symptoms rather than the *cause* of the trouble. A doctor, at the outset, has to rely upon the patient's description of his symptoms to give him just an idea of what the trouble or sickness may be. In spiritual healing on the other hand the patient has not to say anything at all about his illness. The Spirit Guide, through the healer, will unfailingly diagnose the illness without a word being said by the patient.

There have been innumerable instances that have been complied and documented, each bearing testimony to the healing process of patients attending hospitals with their complaints. Pathological investigations and X-rays confirm tumors in the brain, growth in the lungs, bone malformations, tubercular conditions, ulcers and growths in other parts of the body. At this stage, spirit healing is sought and given. And when the condition is again investigated and X-rayed, the trouble is found to have disappeared to the amazement of the medical profession. Without the inherent driving desire to help another to heal, no one can become a good healer. Good healers are generally known to be deeply religious at heart, deriving much of their success from a deep faith in something or the other— either in the Almighty God or in a specific deity or a departed saint. Without this faith no healing is possible. Doubt has a negative effect so far as healing is concerned. Faith, a mysterious mental phenomenon, acts as a link. The concept of faith in the case of intelligent beings works throughout the cosmos. It removes negative thoughts and makes it congenial for the curative processes. No spirit healing takes place unless the cause to disharmony is removed. This is where spirit healing is immeasurably superior to orthodox medical treatment. After all, medical treatment is more often than not concerned with the treatment of the symptoms and not the cause of the trouble. A doctor, at the outset, has to rely upon the patient's description of his symptoms to give him an idea of what the trouble or sickness may be. In spiritual healing the patient does not have to say anything at all about his illness. The Spirit Guide, through the healer, will unfailingly diagnose the illness without a word being said by the patient!

Before the healing forces are set in motion, prayers are offered by the healer. Nothing in the universe takes place by chance and every change is law-governed. "There is no such thing as chance," says Voltaire, "What we call by that name is the effect which we see of a cause which we do not see."

Healing is always a well-planned act. When a patient is deemed to be "incurable" by the medical profession, it is clear that man's scientific wisdom is exhausted. And as the so-called "incurables" are mostly cured, it denotes that a higher intelligence positively comes into the picture. This, once again, proves that this cure can only be through the mind of a spirit-body. The spirit-people have been able to acquire a greater knowledge of both the physical world and the metaphysical laws governing them. This planned effort and use of forces effect the change in the "mind" of the patient, thus leading to the body's cure.

Our bodies are subject to definite laws that control our health from birth to grave. Therefore, a spiritual healing must also be the product of law-governed forces that induce any change. Spiritual healing, I would emphatically state, is not opposed to any medical treatment. On the contrary, it is done with the full assistance and cooperation of the medical profession. It was way back in 1959 that each of the London Hospital Authorities was asked for permission by the National Federation of Spiritual Healers for its accredited members to go into the hospitals for the purpose of administering "healing" when requested by patients. By the end of that year, twenty-two of these authorities granted permission. Today more than three hundred London Hospitals have officially permitted spiritual healers to attend on the patients and comply with their desire to be spiritually healed.

It is thus clear that a pleasant and harmonious form of co-operation now exists between the medical fraternity and spiritual healers. It is time that doctors and surgeons in our country had observed with an open mind the consistent progress made by the patients receiving spiritual healing, so that they became genuinely and quantitatively inclined to welcome this healing for the sick ones under their care. The ideal method of combating disease is to obtain cooperation between the two methods of treatment. They are complementary to each other. The West has accepted this without any reservation or scepticism. I do not see any reason why it should not be so in the East as well and with the same seriousness of purpose.

The *Evidence for Spiritual Healing* by Harry Edwards, published in 1953, is a book that can rightly be called a provocative challenge to all who discount the reality of spirit healing. It features the activities of a man whom many regarded as the world's greatest healer with the largest healing practice in the United Kingdom for over a quarter of a century. Edwards received over a million healing letters annually and every patient who wrote suffered from some kind of "incurable" malady, which he tried to heal *in absentia* with remarkable success. The book contains over 6,000 extracts from case histories of persons who suffered mainly from chronic diseases—-given up by the doctors—showing that supernormal or "miracle" healing had taken place. The object of Harry Edwards's book was to present by the sheer weight of its massive testimony, the irrefutable evidence of Spirit Healing. It cannot be ignored or fail to impress even the most hardened sceptic. It is a chronicle of 10,369 healings in four years through one man and his two associates, of astounding but authentic events ever published. It is worthwhile knowing that the letters pertaining to the case histories are certified by a highly reputable firm of Chartered Accountants of London — Hepburn, Hagley & Knight. As the case histories are scanned, special characteristics can be noted. The first is the relatively high percentage of recoveries among patients upon whom the doctors had earlier pronounced the "sentence of death". Then there is a considerable number of cases in which the illness was thought to be "hopeless" and yet a cure or a substantial benefit had followed the healing.

Another feature connected with the above observation is that many of the patients endured their infirmities for a number of years, sometimes almost a lifetime, without redress from the medical profession. The observing, unbiased mind will see in the testimonies that healing had been received for almost every kind of illness — from paralysis to nervous breakdown, from boils to chronic skin diseases, from tumours to cancer, from mental tension to violence, even insanity. A great majority of the testimonies refers to patients whom the healer had never seen. They had been treated by the absent-healing method, the only contact between the healer and the patient being by letter and these often written by a third party!

It is indeed very interesting to know that some of those who are cured by spirit healing *in absentia* are unaware that they were being helped at all! The testimonies form only a *very* small proportion of the total number of healings that had followed treatment in person from the Harry Edwards Spiritual Sanctuary of England.

In 1945, Harry Edwards submitted that the basic cause behind most forms of skin diseases lay in the nervous tensions and frustrations and that local use of ointments, etc.. was not at all curative. Just two years later, the same fact was claimed by a great medical scientist. So it is with organic diseases, and cancer in particular. In 1957, Harry Edwards published a paper, stating that most forms of cancer, especially cancer of the breast in women, resulted from frustration and inner psychological disturbances. An eminent physician, Sir Heneage Ogilvie, has expressed much later, similar views: "A happy man never gets cancer." In fact, it is not surprising that in a number of cases, where medical treatment had failed, spiritual healing effected the cures. It simply means that use of merely physiological treatment would often fail to achieve results. Where there is a combination of both the methods, the result has been positive. All sicknesses being basically spiritual, it is not surprising that healing may ensue from the application of spiritual methods alone.

These emphatic assertions and facts are meant for those who dismiss out-of-hand the entire concept of spiritual healing because of a lack of holistic knowledge. It is rightly said that prejudice is the commonest of human feelings and an open mind, a rare virtue.

Spiritual healing is a gift of the Spirit. It is an evolved attribute of the human mind. It takes place in consequence of a thought-emission to the world of Spirit. It is the firm conviction of all spiritualists that the law-governed healing rays are projected in an appropriate quantity and quality by a discarnate Spirit having great experience, knowledge and skill.

Spiritual healing is an integral part of evolution, whether it is employed by a personality or some power. Ray Branch, who was Harry Edwards's working colleague and who looked after the latter's Spiritual Healing Sanctuary, has recently concluded a splendid lecture by quoting a simple, quasi-mathematical formula to explain what it all means:

$$\frac{\text{Love + Compassion}}{\text{Attunement}} = \text{Healing Energy}$$

Branch's "chart" centred on the changing scene in the world at large, which concentrated our thoughts on the eternal truth as exemplified in spiritual healing. He was one of the greatest twentieth-century English spiritual healers.

5

Healing is a Science

Birth, life and entry into the realm of the spirit is a part of a plan of majestic splendours. When God has some significant work to do, He appoints His angels or ministers within the heavenly host to do His work, and that is surely the way in which those who are suffering are led towards recovery. The primary purpose of spiritual healing is to eradicate the cause of sickness. It is now accepted that the major part of our adversities is the product of soul and mind disharmony. We progress spiritually by consciously overcoming these. They are not just wiped off the slate. A spiritual cure, therefore, is a healing of any form of sickness and is effected through the spirit agency.

When a complaint is in its early stage, the healing is rapid but when disease becomes deep-rooted, as with chronic arthritis, asthma and cancer, then a prolonged period of treatment is necessary. Often the cure is gradual and yet progressive. This is because the healing follows an orderly process overcoming the cause of disease and then the symptoms, so that in elect spiritual healing is a science and its results are ultimately permanent.

Another aspect of the nature of the healing intelligence is that healings take place only in accordance with the laws that govern this art. For instance, if a hand is amputated, we do not see a now one growing. Healing cannot stop the ageing process nor can it assure permanent life on earth. The healing effort therefore is always circumscribed by the laws of life. The much discussed belief that body and mind are but .two aspects of the same substance is now discarded in favour of their being separate entities. Each has its own capacities, its own tendencies and its own desires. There is no evidence to prove the assumption that every psychological state has a corresponding physical state. Medical investigators have sought, without success, conclusive evidence that this is always the natural state of things. But the post mortem examinations show no evidence of a lesion in the brain to account for a person's insanity! And from that point of view the materialistic theory is based wholly on the assumption that the change in the brain was of a chemical nature, due to perverted metabolism. The doctor prescribes drugs with an aim to restore the normal metabolism and bring the body to its natural healthy equilibrium. The submerged or hidden parts of the mind are in touch with active spiritual beings who play their part in the outstanding cures effected by spiritual healers.

Healers of repute have said from time to time that worry and stress disable us and diminish our efficiency, filling us with apprehension and misgiving. Fear, as a matter of fact, often actually brings into being the object of fear. It would add years to our life and very much to our peace and health if we could stop worrying. Is it not true that in science laboratories it has been demonstrated that emotional stress brings about chemical reactions in different parts of the human body? Emotive causes can produce an actual physical change in the working of the vital tissues. How true are the general rules of health emphasized by the healer: "Keep a quiet, contented mind. Train yourself in the habit of meeting emergency with calmness, never giving away to brooding and worry. Avoid as poisonous and suicidal, hatred, anger and fear."

It is interesting to read what Francis Angold has to say about the characteristics of health and healing: "Medical practice thinks in terms of anatomical structure and organic function. Spiritual healing is concerned with the power of re-creation. Medical science is ever seeking a cure for some specific disease; spiritual healing is devoted to the understanding of the nature of all diseases. Whereas medical science endeavours to provide a pharmaceutical remedy for every known disease, spiritual healing seeks to relate the sufferer to the course of health. When all else fails, orthodox medicine, still thinking in terms of structure and function, removes the offending member or organ. In the last resort, medical practice adopts an attitude of fatalism."

Spiritual Healing, on the other hand, attests to the individuality of human nature. Such healing asserts in the name of the Spirit, the power to heal, even in the direst extremity, every defective member and each inoperative organ. The individuality of health and healing is established when Spirit speaks into Spirit, and existence becomes the interpretation of 'LIFE' ! So long as the healer and, through him, the patient, are attuned to the Divine Source whether, through a Spirit or any denominational faith, then through these agencies affinity is established with God — the Supreme Spirit of love, compassion and grace, and then, within die laws of creation, minds can be soothed and cleansed and bodies can be rid of diseases.

F. Terry Newman has said in *The Spiritual Healer* edited by him (1964): "The successful treatment of a malady by a medical physician frequently results in the patient experiencing a sense of physical well-being. The successful treatment of sickness by a spiritual healer invariably results not only in physical well-being, but in a sense of heightened spiritual awareness. This is true of both physical and psychosomatic disorders. Neither orthodox nor unorthodox healers have, in the literal sense, healed their patients, for though the former has directed material aid and the latter interceded on a non-physical level, both have functioned as selective channels for the operation of different laws, one on a physical, the other on a psycho-spiritual level.

"To the perceptive mind, it is obvious that an ideal state must exist if these two therapies were complementary rather than of independent natures. Both are governed by law, the one natural, the other Divine. This is the fulcrum upon which all our lives are balanced; for though we are Spirits here and now, we live in a physical world where material values are predominant."

Communication from one mind to another without the aid of senses is a fact established through laboratory experiments. It is therefore a fact that our prayers for the sick are also a part of the mental machinery used by the healers to transmit a spiritual power from God to man. God uses the human mind-waves to carry His healing energies to the afflicted ones. In prayer we are not telling God something He does not know already. Healers actually help to establish harmonious relations with God's will. Prayer is not only communion with God but also cooperation with Him. The more we learn to work with God, the more we shall discover that the infinite resources of the Eternal are waiting for us to tap and harness hidden powers for the good of our fellow men.

Spiritual healing is not something apart from religion. It is the practical application of a code of morality which all religious thought engenders. It is a move in the direction of a higher spirituality. It is a fact that some of the world's best-known religions —Hinduism, Christianity, Islam, Buddhism, Judaism and Zoroastrianism — preach about virtues of love towards one another, of compassion for those who suffer, of charity towards die needy, of brotherly love towards all mankind. No religion would condone the conduct of those who permit anger, jealousy, or any form of conduct which would bring suffering to others. The essential quality for spiritual healing can be found in the moral ethics of all religions.

The gift of spiritual healing brings us into close relationship with the basic element of religion. Religion and spiritual healing are manifestations of the universal creative powers. They are a gift of the Spirit. I firmly believe and emphatically assert that spiritual Healing is no longer an abstract mystery. It is a spirit science based on knowledge and understanding. It is a recognisable gift. It is the fulfilment of God's commandment to heal the sick. All healing therefore has its origin in the Divine. It is God's gift to His chosen instruments, irrespective of race or religion. It is not the possession or monopoly of any one religion.

When we observe a spiritual healing taking place, a painful condition of long standing disappearing, a growth dispersing as if by magic, sight and hearing being restored and so on, we would like to know how it was accomplished. There must be a reason for all things, and any state of change can only come from the application of law-governed forces, but in considering how healings come, one is faced with a fundamental difficulty. This difficulty is that we can only understand that which is within our knowledge to comprehend. For example, it is quite impossible to give a person, who has been blind since birth, any description of a colour, for he cannot visualise what he has not seen. So it is with spiritual healing. Because healing comes from the non-material dimensions of the Spirit, it is impossible for us to even visualise something that is not physical. Therefore, the full understanding of how healings take place is not available. But is it at all necessary? Yet, every healing is a planned act and therefore it needs some kind of intelligence to carry it out. It can only take place, I repeat, within the laws that govern us. The spirit intelligence has the wisdom of knowing how to direct forces within the law to bring about a radical change for the better.

Healing is not time-governed by our standards. It is not as if healing is like medicine that has to be taken every three or four hours! It is a continuous process functioning according to the patient's needs and urgency. There is never any one set answer to any question concerning spiritual healing. There have been many instances when a telephone call or a special request has been made to overcome a particular condition. These requests do become part of a special intercession and it so often follows that immediate relief is forthcoming of which the patient has had no knowledge at all. This is a remarkably challenging feat!

Spiritual healers have a great responsibility towards their patients and likewise patients have a great responsibility towards their healers — both have a great responsibility towards God. Healing power never resides in human bodies. Healing influences are directed through the healer. Faith in healing is helpful inasmuch as it helps the patient psychologically but faith is not imperative. If it were so, infants, animals and third party healings could not take place successfully. God is undoubtedly a God of

Love. But love, by its very nature, does its healing work more effectively and more naturally in a heart which is receptive or responsive and in a mind which accepts the demands of that same love.

A healer may not cure every disease or every patient whom he may treat. Let us not forget that no form of therapy, however modern, has a monopoly of cures. Each therapy has its successes and its failures. Spiritual Healing, however, has a far better cure rate than any other therapy, because it treats causes rather than symptoms. Most orthodox treatments relieve symptoms but leave the cause untouched. It is accepted even in medical circles that most diseases 'are psychosomatic. Whatever drug you administer to the body, it cannot get at the root cause — the mind — even though it may succeed in allaying the symptoms temporarily. Whatever the trouble, the life-force which is the Spirit, will utilise all the means within its power to restore health. Real health is achieved when there is a natural harmony between body, mind and spirit. Through the healer, there flows a power — which we believe is Divine — that stimulates the patient's life-force and encourages it to perform its task of recuperation. The healer is merely a channel. There is evidence that the healer cooperates with doctors and surgeons who are no longer in this world and who are far more intelligent and who have greatly progressed on the other side and who continue to use their rich experience and talents through instruments called healers on this side. There is no doubt that two of Britain's most famous healers, Gordon Turner and Ray Branch, are actually helped by outstanding men just as Harry Edwards was helped by Pasteur and Lister. According to the spiritualists, the spirits of some departed doctors, determined to help humanity develop it as a regular science, are working very hard in the beyond ("*Pitruloka*" of the *Upanishads*) and co-operating with spiritually developed media who can pass on spiritual energy to patients as it is supplied to them without injuring their own health in any way.

By this brand of healing, some of. the worst and most cruel excesses of the maximum-effort treatment developed in the West, are expected to be removed, and India, the propounder of Karmic laws and of the concept of reincarnation (see Johannes Von Butler, Journey to Infinity, Fontana 1971), is expected to take a leading role in the propagation of this developing branch of medicine.

That yoga and meditation are already so popular in the West and coming East again via the West, is already a clear indication of the pattern of things to come.

6

The Efficacy of Spiritual Healing

There are very few who really have faith — that complete trust — in healing and its gradual and progressive results. Most of the patients resort to healing when there is no hope left for their survival. It is therefore necessary to educate die people and make diem conscious of the fact that psychic healing is not only as effective as any other treatment, but sometimes it is, to a great extent, even superior to other forms of orthodox treatment. The very fact that the Harry Edwards Spiritual Healing Sanctuary in England was recognised by a person like Sir Winston Churchill speaks of the efficacy of the therapy.

There are more than 3,000 spiritual healers in the United Kingdom. *The Journal of the National Federation of Spiritual Healers and International Fellowship of Healing* has published three interviews — one of them with a leading physicist — on spiritual healing. On the lines of these interviews, our views are conditioned by science (mainly physical science); but there is tremendous time lag and present beliefs are based on earlier physics while physics has progressed towards more integral views of our world of material and para-material components.

On this basis, we should move towards a holistic view of the physical, psychological and spiritual approaches to health as well as living in general. In London, more and more hospitals have been seeking the help of spiritual healers, but this they do in good time, before the patients are beyond recovery. In India, spiritual healing is not yet projected properly to the public. It is essentially the work of the journalists to interview the healers and study their work, so that suitable reporting is done with an open mind, and maximum publicity is given to the healers' work. This is how suffering humanity would be able to cultivate adequate faith in and knowledge about the possibilities and limitations of spiritual healing.

I had tremendous difficulty in convincing the journalists who in the beginning just refused to deal with me. Later, some came to me of their own accord because one of the patients who was cured of a very serious illness (degeneration of the spinal cord with acute lumbar and cervical spondylitis along with arthritis of all the joints) happened to be one of the Directors of one of the most important groups of newspaper publications in India. It was because of him that one of the editors sought my interview which was published in 1975. However, the editor was extremely cautious and very particular about going through all my case histories and contacting some patients in order to substantiate my claims. It was only when he was fully satisfied — and also because he knew of the Director's obvious recovery — that the editor published my interview. But I am sorry to say that full justice was not done to my work as both the summing up as also the introduction were punctuated with hints of scepticism! However, the ice was broken by one important editor making it easy for me to attract others who came to me after trying me out with health problems of their own relatives, suffering from different diseases — specially schizophrenia. The Bombay Doordarshan interview also materialised because of several articles written by my grateful patients published in papers all over the country. Moreover, an increasing number of patients who sought healing help, spoke out about their recovery. I cannot help reproducing one write-up — only a part of it — by Mrs. Singh that appeared in one of the November 1978 issues of *Economic Times*.

"In Bombay, reactions to such psychic phenomena are often sceptical — 'hallucinations', 'auto-suggestion' or 'psychosomatic cures' are about the range of rationalisations that are offered. Yet the thousands who flock in for the healing touch and are cured do not wish their names to be divulged — an attitude typical of the urban 'intelligentsia'." Dr. R. K. Keni is perhaps the only psychic healer who is a practising physician as well. Attached to the Bombay Hospital, Dr. Keni's initiation into the realm of faith healing is interesting.

"What strikes one about his Consulting Room at the Bombay Hospital is that instead of the usual antiseptic odour, there is an all-pervading smell of an unseen incense. On the left, as one enters, is a small revolving stool where the treatment is given and on the wall above it is a painting — a flame-like representation of his Guide.

"The doctor himself is quite unlike one's concept of a faith healer, clad in the usual medical practitioner's attire, he has a practical and likable disposition. However, his piercing brown eyes behind the horn-rimmed glasses can be quite disconcerting to a hard-bound sceptic. It is not a comfortable feeling to know that someone is aware of your ailments without being told of them. Within the first fifteen minutes he had correctly diagnosed mine...."

Many ask me whether ministers, lawyers, really intelligent persons and atheists have ever come to me. My answer is once again an emphatic YES. Not only ministers, not only lawyers, but two top barristers, a number of foreigners, top people in the film industry, prominent journalists, leading doctors and surgeons, important industrialists and reputed people in the teaching profession — all have visited me. I do not know whether they are atheists or not. But even after being cured if some of them prefer to call themselves atheists, I would call them hypocrites! May God help such people! I have a long list of such very important people with their names and addresses. I do not reveal the identity of such important people because they do not wish me to do so and the reason for this is best known to them! It is indeed difficult to say why a very important minister and well-known author, who suffered from acute cervical spondylitis which made him use a belt round his neck for years and which deprived him of the pleasure of driving, wanted to remain anonymous. He was cured of his pain in less than three months and he can now drive without any discomfort. And there is the case of a very important and internationally known journalist who too suffered from cervical and lumbar spondylitis. She too was cured in less than two months. She too can now drive her car easily. Yet she has not made any effort to write about her experiences with a healer! There is yet another case of a minister who managed the finances of our country. He suffered from irratic hypertension and a weak heart. He was cured in less than two months but he was very particular about remaining incognito. Why this attitude? Others in my place might have called it cowardice but I do not wish to offer any comments. On the other hand there is the striking example of a fiery M.P., a very intelligent and versatile personality, who after being cured was honest enough not to remain incognito. She even sent me more patients from Delhi. Her name is Mrs. Tarkeshwari Sinha. I wish there were many such gracious persons.

I have on my list one particular industrialist who also owns a chain of English and other language publications in India— a very influential man who was cured sooner by healing than by medical therapy and he too was most particular about keeping his name a secret. In addition to this, I did not get a single letter from him, either thanking me for the help or acknowledging my letter enquiring after his health! Well, there are patients and patients. There are some who are grateful, loyal, with a lot of understanding, always ready to cooperate and help. But there are others who come with great selfishness in their mind, fearful, full of doubts. They come because they are forced to come by someone or the other who was cured by healing. You see a marked feeling on their faces as they narrate their ailment with negative thoughts. They are sure they would never be cured. They are nevertheless cured in spite of all their negative attitude and distrust. But the cure does not make any difference as far as their attitude is concerned. They go out and boast of their cure through a clinic at Boston or a super specialist in the United States! This attitude does not hamper the good work because a healer-doctor is basically concerned with his duty and his efforts, irrespective of the reactions of patients. The most pitiable are those patients who come to my consulting rooms with chronic diseases. They are amongst those who have spent a fortune (and months and years of their time) in seeking a cure. They have suffered enough, and more. They have given enough of their time to their doctors. They are in the worst possible condition — "beyond repairs"—and yet when it comes to psychic healing, they are not prepared to wait patiently for the cure. They need a guarantee. They are extremely curious. They ask you all sorts of questions about the treatment. They, in short, expect only a miracle. The cure should be *now* — instantaneous and permanent. They expect the healer to be another Jesus Christ and cure their chronic, deep-rooted, incurable ailments with a mere touch! They are not prepared to take psychic healing as seriously as medical healing. For them one is a scientific approach, and the other is a matter of coincidence!

Dr. Horace Leaf has quoted a striking example of this kind of attitude. A member of the Stock Exchange presented himself at a Spiritual Healing Clinic, saying challengingly, with a cynical smile, to the practitioner, "I understand you can perform miracles. Well, I have for eighteen months been under the care of three Harley Street specialists with a pain in my right knee which makes my life almost unbearable, and they have done me no good. Can you do something?" His attitude was that of a man about to make a doubtful investment with the chances of it turning into a bad one, heavily loaded. Dr. Horace Leaf cured him in less than five minutes with the aid of "his spiritual helper". "How do you feel now?" he asked. "Absolutely free from pain," and the patient demonstrated the fact by walking smartly up and down the Consulting Room. "Good", smilingly said Dr. Leaf, extending his hand in farewell. "You will be allright".

"Oh", returned the amazed patient, stamping his leg to try it out once more. "I am too old a bird to believe this," and took his a little-too-puzzling departure.

Many human beings are sceptical, not because they lack in intelligence but because they are ignorant. To such people I would like to say that psychic or spiritual healing is not only an art but it is also a perfect science with a better and higher cure ratc authentically recorded for anyone to look into seriously and honestly.

"Doctor, is it necessary for you to record names and addresses of persons you treat? Could I not be an exception?"

The father of a 23-year-old daughter suffering from schizophrenia asked me. And so did others whose daughters had asthma, leucoderma, venereal diseases, epilepsy and sterility. In such cases I do understand the parents' anxiety, hesitation and fears because the girls have to be married and in India any effort on my part to publicise their names would positively come in the way of matrimony and cause considerable harm. But I wonder why people who are very well settled in life should be so secretive when diseases like migraine or spondylitis, loss of hair or rhinitis are cured by a psychic healer's dedicated efforts. It is strange but practically every second patient wishes to remain anonymous. Why should such an attitude prevail? Do they do a similar thing when they are healed in a "modern" hospital? There have been exceptions though. One sensible girl, who came from Pune with a cancer in her breast, was treated successfully, and, in grateful acknowledgement, she *did* allow me to publicise her name and address in the press!

There was a similar case of a doctor who went into acute bouts of depression, almost bordering on schizophrenia. It took him four months to be normal. He too permitted me to use his name and address as and when I wished. I did this twice when I was interviewed by two well-known magazines.

I cannot help being a bit amused when I recall two other patients, one of whom was born with six fingers and an equal number of toes. He said, "I shall consider you a genuine Psychic Healer if the extra fingers and toes are removed without surgery." It is not necessary to repeat what I said to him. Another patient whose hand was amputated after an accident, expected me—and quite seriously—to replace it by healing— no matter how much money it cost him! I must therefore admit that these two and similar cases simply do not belong to our healing provinces.

7

The Unknown Factors which Operate Mysteriously

Psychological research has established that the average human being uses only a very small percentage of his potential. In crisis, his body can and does summon incredible reserves that enable him to achieve fantastic feats that are regarded impossible, normally. The human mind is even more remarkable. According to F. Terry Newman, a noted psychic author: "The history of civilisation is starred like a galaxy with its achievements. Guided by good, it has approached divinity and conversely, by depravity, evil."

The human mind is unquestionably the link between our body and Spirit. The finest achievements have always been inspired by the Spirit when we have chosen to progress in close affinity with nature. Newman says: "Whenever Spirit has taken a path leading away from nature, from natural things, it has proved a barren and fruitless journey. Much of modern civilisation, instead of being complementary to nature, has deviated into unnatural ways of life."

It is a fact that the late Dr. B. C. Roy's healing abilities were supernatural. He would diagnose a so-called incurable case with an uncanny certainty which was so characteristic of that great doctor (he was also the Chief Minister of Bengal and an outstanding figure in the world of politics.). Once a patient was under his treatment, even a difficult disease would disappear in no time. There are innumerable instances of healing miracles by

Dr. B. C. Roy. Like him, many a good doctor knows that not the whole of his success can be rationalised by known and accepted scientific norms: there are, more often than generally recognised, cases where the correct diagnosis has come in a flash. But few doctors would freely admit the existence of the still unknown factors that operate mysteriously to bring about the progress and recovery of individual patients.

Matter and mind are complementary and hence a frame of reference suited only to the observation of matter cannot deal with problems of mind and/or Spirit. Similarly, a study of mere physical relationship by physical methods cannot enlighten us regarding psychic or spiritual phenomena. I am more than convinced of this.

"The richest field for new discoveries is the odd, unclassified recidium," says William James.

Similarly Sir George Thompson has said: "It is the greatest discovery in method that science has made that the apparently trivial, the merely curious, may be clues to the understanding of the deepest principle of nature."

But much more important than this is what T. N. Huxley says: "I am unaware of anything that has a right to the title of an impossibility except a contradiction in terms."

If someone had spoken about the wonders of electronics a few years ago, who would have believed it! Similarly the matter of astronauts landing on the moon would have been considered a fairy tale! Galileo and many others before and after him were persecuted for the principles which have been later accepted as scientific and by which the scientists of today will swear.

Dr. Rhinehart of the U.S. had to do many experiments on para-psychological findings not only on qualitative basis but on a statistical basis indicating the probability, statistically calculated, of the related phenomena being due to (i) specific legitimate causes on the one hand and (ii) pure chance on the other. It is this that put the scientific world on the defensive and these phenomena are now gradually being accepted as realistic, even though we may not be able to explain them in familiar terms. Does this not indicate that we should be more open-minded rather than dogmatic? Some facts may not fit in with current notions, but how can it justify an "ostrich"stand to deny them? In fact, Einstein formulated his theory of relativity after long and arduous work on the basis of small discrepancies not taken note of seriously by other scientists before. If we fail to consider such questions as relevant, we cannot claim to have a scientific attitude! If so, established facts in psychic healing and psychic surgery, however seemingly incredible to science so far, should be accepted as a challenge by research and not rejected out of hand just because it is familiar knowledge. In any case this would not be scientific attitude. Science is characterised by known factors or factual data leading to formulation of hypotheses which can explain diverse phenomena by progressively simpler laws with verification and use, even for predictions. This was simple in physical sciences but became more complex for biological sciences and still more for social sciences where the variables are so many that formulation and verification on these lines requires use of statistics and probabilities.

"Lord, what these mortals be," Shakespeare put this comment into the mouth of one of his characters. We compliment ourselves on the excellence of technological achievements of our scientific progress. We have enthroned science as our true God, encouraged nuclear discoveries that have produced the greatest question mark in history threatening the fate of civilisation. We butcher millions of living creatures 'scientifically' to find wonder drugs for a number of diseases which are ever increasing. Illnesses have multiplied themselves due to side-effects which have become worse than the diseases themselves. In spite of all these achievements, by and large, the majority of people find that peace, happiness, serenity, good health and confidence elude them and they are confronted with frustration, anxieties and fears.

"I am a Doctor of Medicine, loyal to my profession and full of all of a doctor's traditions which may easily become prejudices.

But I am bound to say from my own knowledge that there are psychic avenues towards cures which reach their aim when mere physical ones fail", Sir Arthur Conan Doyle said that. He was himself a fantastic healer who was an expert on intuitive diagnosis.

It is not only a pity but a disastrous thing that today, religion no longer enjoys the respect it enjoyed in olden days. We have divorced ourselves from nature and thus are not able to enjoy its life-giving foods and fruits. We devitalise food products with colouring, additives and preserves. We spray the crops with poison and foul the atmosphere we breathe. We drink gallons of medicine and swallow a mountain of pills, yet we mistake the symptoms for the effect. We chase illusion and miss the reality.

Shakespeare was right. Although we have wrested from nature so many secrets, we are profoundly ignorant about ourselves. If facts and events about psychic healing are presented to us for which no explanation is forthcoming from science established so far, we react by denying the phenomena, prejudicially labelling them miracles and therefore chimerical. Such biased attitude of running away from facts in a self-blinding nescience contradicts the temper of truth. In fact, the very science that we adore and in whose name we neglect and persecute new phenomena, accepts these phenomena when we are rendered helpless and have no option but to accept it! However, a minority has found the beginnings of the answers that elude the majority. They have discovered the truth about life and themselves by becoming acquainted with spiritual foundation upon which the whole of existence rests.

Today there are ample evidences with regard to the benefits of psychic healing at first hand which are verifiable for anyone who profess a scientific attitude. With regard to the scientific attitude, there are two significant facts.

a) The patients do not claim total relief but only practical relief indicating absence of just blind faith or purely suggestive good efforts.

b) Quite apart from the relief, the fact that a healer is able to cure—completely or partially, such patients as are given up by medical profession as "incurables"—is a force to be recognised apart from its explanation.

Besides, it is for the common public who are concerned with relief and not with the theories to judge where scientific or established benefits lie. Hence today psychic healing, psychic surgery, ectoplasmic formations, multiform med-iumistic powers, trances, seances, astral projections, para-nomical experiences, materialisation and telepathic reading are establishing themselves and even helping humanity to a very great extent. It is for science to widen its scope and prove or disprove these phenomena, and meanwhile to keep an open mind. For even in established science, the line between the material and the non-material, the organic and the inorganic is growing dim; so too is the partition between physics and metaphysics, nature and supernature.

8

Some Other Issues

There has been elaborate research done on psychic phenomena since the fifteenth century by such eminent people like Sir Oliver Lodge, Arthur Koestler, Dr. Carl Wickland, Edgar Wallace, Hannen Swaffer, Sir Arthur Eddington, Dr. Endlicher, M. Wilhelm Hochstetter, Dr. Neid, M. Constantin Delhez, Dr. Huss, David Hume, Franz Anton Mesmer, Mary Baker Eddy and many other internationally known personalities, some of whom were renowned scientists and philosophers.

It is indeed painful to note that the medical world is nevertheless prejudiced against the existence of wider scientific (let alone spiritual) possibilities.

Even the great philosopher, Arthur Schopenhauer, had come to the conclusion in the mid-1800s that the operation of cause and effect was only one aspect of the world. In the tiny world of the atomic nucleus, the cause and effect must exist in some unique way other than in gross phenomena.

It is therefore not right to apply laws of the gross to psychological and spiritual spheres.

It has been proved that mind can no longer be regarded as a rare and recent phenomenon. The mind is an intrinsic part of everything that IS and WAS. There is no justification to disbelieve the powers that operate beyond the barriers of time and space.

Has it not been convincingly proven by Maharshis who have demonstrated the power of mind over physical functions, and which has also been confirmed by scientists like Einstein and Schweitzer?

Today spiritualism is aided by enormous evidences in spiritual healing, astral projections, materialisation, spirit photography, direct writing and drawing, clairvoyance and clairaudience, trance-speaking, automatic writing, apparitions, impersonation and many other psychic experiments which are mentioned even by such eminent sages like Swami Yogananda and Shri Aurobindo Ghosh and recorded in authentic books of the West, many of them by eminent men of unimpeachable character.

Although some scientists have now accepted spiritualism committed to humanity, there are others who are obstinately biased. This unscientific attitude and closed mind does hinder considerably the larger cause of human well-being.

Alfred Russel Wallace, whose name stands like a landmark as an author and researcher, says in his book *Miracles and Modern Spiritualism* first published in 1878: "... I have heard stated in public, and received with applause that it requires immense scientific knowledge to decide on the reality of any uncommon or incredible facts and that till scientific men investigate and prove them, they are not worthy of credit. Now I venture to say that a greater fallacy than this was never put forth. The subject is very important, and the error is very common, but fact is the exact opposite of what is stated; for I assert, without fear of contradiction, that whenever the scientific men of any age have denied the facts of investigators on a priori grounds, they have always been wrong." It is not necessary to do more than refer to the famous names of Galileo, Harvey and Jenner. The great discoveries they made were, as we know, violently opposed by all their contemporary scientists, to whom they appeared absurd and incredible; but we have equally striking examples much nearer to our own day. When Benjamin Franklin brought the subject of lightning conductors before the Royal Society, he was laughed at as a dreamer, and his paper was not admitted to the Philosophical Transactions. When Dr. Young put forth his wonderful proofs of the undulatory theory of light, he was hooted at as absurd by the popular scientific writers of the day. *The Edinburgh Review* called upon the public to put Thomas Gray into a straitjacket for maintaining the practicability of railroads. Sir Humphrey Davy laughed at the idea of London ever being lighted with gas. When Stephenson proposed to use locomotives on the Liverpool and Manchester Railway, learned men gave evidence that it was impossible that they could go even twelve miles an hour. Another great scientific authority declared it to be equally impossible for ocean steamers ever to cross the Atlantic. The French Academy of Sciences ridiculed the great astronomer Arago, when he wanted merely to discuss the subject of the electric telegraph. Medical men ridiculed the stethoscope when it was first discovered. Painless operations during mesmeric coma were pronounced impossible and therefore impostures.

But one of the most striking instances — one of the most recent cases of this opposition to, or rather disbelief in facts opposed to the current belief of the day, among men who are generally charged with going too far in the other direction— is that of the doctrine of the "Antiquity of man". Boue, an experienced French geologist, in 1823, discovered a human skeleton in eight-feet deep, hardened mud of the Rhine. It was sent to the great anatomist Cuvier, who so utterly discredited the fact that he threw aside this invaluable fossil as worthless, and it was lost. Sir C. Lyell, from personal investigation on the spot, now believes that the statements of the original observer were quite accurate.

As early as 1715 flint weapons were found with the skeleton of an elephant in an excavation in Gray's Inn Lane, in the presence of Conyers, who placed them in the British Museum, where they remained utterly unnoticed till quite recently. In 1800 Mr. Frere found flint weapons along with the remains of extinct animals at Hoxne, in Suffolk. From 1841 to 1846, the celebrated French geologist, Boucher de Perthes, discovered great quantities of flint weapons in the drift gravels of North of France; but for many years he could convince none of his fellow scientists that they were works of art, or worthy of the slightest attention. At length, however, in 1853, he began to make converts. In 1859-60, some of the most eminent geologists visited the spot, and fully confirmed the truth of his observations and deductions.

Another branch of the subject was, if anything, given still worse treatment. In 1825, Mr. McEnery of Torquay discovered worked flints along with the remains of extinct animals in the celebrated Kent's Hole Cavern; but the account of his discoveries was simply laughed at. In 1840, one of the first geologists, Mr. Godwin Austen, brought this matter before the Geological Society, and Mr. Vivian, of Torquay, sent in a paper fully confirming Mr. McEnery's discoveries, but it was thought too improbable to be published. Fourteen years later, the Torquay Natural Society made further observations, entirely confirming the previous ones, and sent an account of them to the Geological Society of London; but the paper was rejected, as too improbable for publication. Now, however, for the past five years the cave has been systematically explored under the superintendence of a Committee of the British Association, and all the previous reports for forty years have been confirmed, and have been shown to be even more wonderful than in reality. It may be said that "this was proper scientific caution". Perhaps it was; but at all events it proves this important fact that in this, as in every other case, the humble and often unknown observers have been right; the men of science who reject their observations have been wrong.

Let us consider the phenomena termed supernatural and incredible. Are these less worthy of attention than those that have been quoted above? Clairvoyance for instance is still "unscientific". The people who have observed clairvoyance, and have scrupulously tested it through long, long years, will rank in scientific knowledge and in intellectual ability as quite equal to the observers in any other branch of science. There are seven such competent medical men — Dr. Elliotson, Dr. Gregory, Dr. Esdaile, Dr. Lee, Dr. Ashburner, Dr. Herbert Mayo and Dr. Hadlock besides persons of such high integrity and intellect as Miss Martineu, H. G. Atkinson, Charles Bray and Baron

Reichenbach. With the history of the previous discoverers before us, is it more likely that these people of high ability, knowing all the arguments against the facts and investigating them carefully, should be all wrong, and those who say a priori that the thing is impossible should be all right, or the contrary?

The whole history of the progress of human knowledge shows us, that the disputed prodigy of one age becomes the accepted natural phenomenon of the next and the many apparent miracles have been due to laws of nature subsequently discovered.

We know so little of what nerve or life-force really is, how it acts or can act, and in what degree is it capable of transmission from one human being to another, that it would be indeed rash to affirm that under no exceptional conditions could phenomena, such as the apparently miraculous cure of many diseases, or perception through other channels than the ordinary senses, ever take place.

Reality can be apprehended in its many facts only by tools and technologies adequate for each situation. It is certainly not a scientific attitude for men of the medical and the scientific world to refuse to investigate established facts just because they are 'new'.

It is a proven fact that even while the body is at rest during sleep, the soul life is active. There are many who have deep insight into the soul's activity — a fact which has been proved over and over again. If the soul life, which relates us to the Infinite Spirit, is always active even while the body is at rest, why cannot the mind or soul direct conditions for improvement in body and mind?

Rev. Thomas Maddock, a leading spiritualist living in Tasmania, who is preaching, lecturing and doing psychic healing, says that Russia spends n million pounds sterling annually on psychic research. The University of Western Australia has accepted healing as an established and fully effective therapy. Our universities should now take up this study seriously — especially in view of our spiritual heritage blended with scientific training.

In the United Kingdom, the United States of America, Brazil, Mexico, Australia and many advanced countries, many of the leading private hospitals have a healing sanctuary attached where the so-called incurables are left to the care of and treatment by the healers.

It is high time we too explored this in our country and harness such a vast reserve of power for human welfare. It is also my earnest desire that healing groups and associations should be as active in our country and in our hospitals as they are in almost all the Western countries. It is my sincere wish that psychic and spiritual healing and orthodox medical treatment should become complementary, so that doctors and healers could work together to bring about fruitful results. Man is undoubtedly a spiritual being in every sense of the word. Man's mind extends beyond the normal needs of his material world to non-physical states. The submerged or the hidden parts of the mind are in touch with active spiritual beings who play their part in bringing about remarkable cures — all of these, authentic — made by spiritual healers. The body is merely the instrument through which the human mind is able to experience the terrene world of ours.

We should be thankful to the labours and the most heroic fortitude of a large number of eminent people who have stood bravely for the establishment of the fact that spiritual healing is the most significantly effective force and this they have proved beyond any doubt and in the face of hostility. It is of course not a new revelation so much as a re-emergence of something as old as humanity itself. One of the exponents of the cause was the great Lord Brougham who in the fifties of the last century uttered an oft quoted remark regarding Modern Spiritualism and its purpose as he rightly compared it to the rising of a rain-cloud in the skies of scepticism.

John Scott, the most familiar name in the spiritual world, has been one of the outstanding writers. He was highly sceptical of any psychic faculty until it manifested in his own self when he received striking communications in automatic writing and then came across overwhelming evidence confirmed by mediums who did not know him (as it happened in my own case) that the communicator was none other than the man known on earth as Lord Curzon—famous as statesman and administrator.

There are hundreds of books with observations and evidences proving convincingly the presence of one of the most potent forces: spiritual healing. These books with the authors' sincere and elaborate research for decades give us more and more convincing details and insight into what has been called "the great unknown force".

> One good experiment is of more value than the ingenuity of a brain like Newton's. Facts are more useful when they contradict, than when they support, received theories.
>
> —*Sir Humphrey Davy*

> The perfect observer in any department of science will have his eyes, as it were, opened, that they may be struck at once by any occurrence which, according to received theories, ought not to happen, for these are the facts which serve as clues to new discoveries.
>
> —*Sir John Herschell*

9

The Power of Thought and the Healing Minute

It is now being extensively recognised that thought is not just an abstract element. Thought is an organised form of potential energy. If a number of people of different races and tongues were to join together in sending out the thought of a rose, it would be the same irrespective of language, and the form of energy from each one could be similar so that if it could be recorded on a disc, like sounds are done, they would be identical. It is not true that whereas one cotton strand is easily broken, when a number of strands are joined together as in a strong rope, the breaking strain could be tremendous? It turns out to be a gigantic force as a result of increasing efforts of a large number of people coming together spontaneously. So it is that when a number of people join collectively at one particular time to send out a combined thought force for peace and healing, there is a built-up effort of tremendous strength and purpose.

This is just what happens every evening for one minute, day in and day out, when on the Home Service, the B.B.C. radios out the chimes of Big Ben. It is a signal for the maximum number of people to put down what they are doing and to enter into the silence of prayer, seeking for others the balm of healing from Spirit, to reach them, and for the guidance of national destinies to maintain harmony, understanding and peace within the world.

Many experiments have proved from time to time that thoughts are tangible things and when there is harmony between transmission and reception, then other people can become conscious of the thoughts that are sent out. It is also a proven fact that we have knowledge about the existence of harmony between ourselves and the heavenly bodies. It is clear that when such efforts are made, die spiritual direction of the thoughts of the observers of "the minute" are received by them.

Harry Edwards—the world's number one healer — has rightly said: "Every cotton strand in a rope is individual, so is every personal thought strand linked together during the healing minute, thus providing the means through which the healing forces can flow to and contact a sick one. Thus the Healing Minute is not simply an abstract exercise but a positive linking up with Spirit, in a characterised way. This is how Absent Healing works. It has purpose. It is constructive. It is directive."

From time to time we read strange things given out as truth. It was once said of truth, "Oh! What crimes are committed in your name!" In an American paper appeared an article written by a London Roman Catholic priest, in which he affirmed that witchcraft was prevalent in Britain (a thoroughly absurd statement) and he ended his article by saying: "Some witches in Britain believe that their mass incantations in the war forced Adolf Hitler to abandon plans to invade England."

What happened is recorded history. In the dark days that followed Dunkirk, Mr. Winston Churchill restored the chiming of Big Ben just before the News on the Home Service, and the whole nation was called to pray, each night as Big Ben chimed, for help to reach the forces of right. In this way the Healing Minute came to be accepted as a part of Britain's life. It is thought by many that it was in response to Divine influencing that Hitler changed his war plans and turned his eyes to the East instead of the West. It was purely a national effort of prayer and certainly not the work of witches!

We in our country have neither a Big Ben nor a fixed prayer minute and yet we could all join together in potential number and fix up say 10 p.m. at the stroke of which just a minute could be observed in silence for providing the means through which the healing forces can flow to and contact the sick ones. It should be a significantly important minute—a signal for the maximum number of people to put down what they may be doing, no matter where they are or what they are doing at that time— to enter into the silence of sincere prayer, seeking for the sick the effect of healing from the Spirit to reach them all. This must be an organised effort for the welfare of the mentally and physically sick.

Life would be dull if it was deprived of any changes to which man must adjust himself. Is it not a fact that human progression in all fields of thought and activity comes through change and adaptability to change? This is an indisputable truth. It is when people of good intention allow thoughts of ordinary matters to fade down and let spiritual directives ascend and become dominant for just 60 seconds that attunement is established in the heavenly realm. In these seconds of attunement and rapport, a more intimate affinity prevails for the Divine healing forces to flow and overcome imperfections and die undesirable disease in the body or mind. Good Health is perfect harmony and happiness. Therefore, when in these 60 seconds of the day we all join together in seeking harmony with the Divine grace, we cannot, indeed help receiving ample spiritual health and strength with which healing too comes in abundant measure to those who are suffering mentally and physically. When countless people join together at this fixed time, it must mean that there is built up a potential force which reaches upwards to God in strength. As this force flows outward, so also will it return surely, giving inner upliftment, strength and health, easing tensions and stresses, restoring energies and bringing peace. This way of profiting is open to each and every one if only you will enter into the good company of thousands of others who make up perhaps the largest family in the world, coming together at one time—for just one 'minute'. Moreover, as we ally with this force through spiritual invocation, we become attuned to a mighty power which is capable of overcoming all sickness. Thoughts are things. Right thinking is the prerogative of all who have the will to harness their thoughts to the things that matter.

The best things in life do not cost money: the smell of new mown grass in our fields, the love for the flowers and animal kingdom, the birds and butterflies, kind thoughts and remembrances, a prayer for the sick.... So it is with this great and noble movement. It costs no money but just one minute of each day and there can be no man or woman—even those who are our rulers—who cannot freely give one minute for healing, to soothe the sick and for peace to be with all of them and with all of us too.

10

Spirits do indicate Useful Events

On first thoughts the future presents only a black and this can be revealed only by unfolding time. The French Philosopher Henri Bergson, who linked time with creation itself, says: "Duration is the continuous progress of the past which gnaws into the future. Each moment is something unforeseeable."

However, psychic facts amply prove that the future is foreseeable but only under certain conditions. The exploration of the future has always held a great fascination for some. There are various modes of such future telling. They are either by the fall of cards or by astrological devices. They are also possible by mathematical probabilities and by dreams or by the psychic awareness of certain sensitivities. Intuitions also play a very important part.

Many people—both wise and stupid—deny the possibility of a prediction. It has all along been a matter of personal predilection. But when one does meet with accurate foretelling in one's own life, one's thoughts on the nature of the Universe are positively affected. There is a very interesting American case of Spencer Thornton (which has received ample publicity)—an amateur magician and a prominent Doctor who worked his way through medical school by demonstrating his talents. He was not psychic and because of his bag of tricks, was sceptical of anyone who claimed to be one. But gradually he was caught up in his own development of ESP. Most of the cases quoted, though gimmicky, are nonetheless evidence of accurate prophecy. Asked by a television network to pick the winner of the Kentucky Derby, Thornton, after scanning the list of runners, he made his selection four days before the race and in the presence of a group of impeccably sincere and honest witnesses. His slip of paper was sealed—unread—in an envelope and placed in the a Bank Vault. He not only foretold the first three horses, but also mentioned the fact of the "photo-finish" for the winner! There is no doubt that events-that-are-to-come do cast their influence on these psychic predictions; the "indications" are clear and full of guidance. They are fore-warnings if only they are accepted in good faith. However, they are in my view discernible to the privileged few.

Richard Wagner had many mystical experiences.. In his autobiography he writes: "The emotions of terror and the dread of ghosts formed quite an important factor in the development of my mind. From my earliest childhood certain mysterious and uncanny things exercised an enormous influence over me." At 17, he suddenly acquired a passion for gambling. One night, he lost nearly everything — even his mother's pension of which he was trustee. In deep despair he gambled his last healer —and won! From then on he could not lose. He risked the most hazardous stake, for it suddenly dawned upon him that this was destined to be his last day with the cards.

"My sensations during the whole of this process were of the most sacred nature," related Wagner. "I felt as if God and his Angels were standing by my side and were whispering words of warning and consolation into my ears." From that moment, gambling lost all fascination for him.

The only other gambling experience in Wagner's life came years later when he went to look for a friend at a Casino. "When a new round of roulette began, I said to him in a voice of quiet certainty 'Number u will win' and it did. I added fuel to the fire of his astonishment at this stroke of good luck by predicting number 27 for the next round. Certainly I remember being overcome by a spell as I spoke, and my number was in fact again victorious." His astonished friend urged him to stake something himself on the numbers which he foretold, but Wagner refused to do so, replying, "As soon as I introduce my own personal interests into the game, my gift of prophecy will disappear at once."

Kenkule von Stradonitz, the German chemist responsible for two important discoveries in Chemistry, viz., the Structure Theory and the Formula for Benzine, said that both these discoveries actually came to him. The former was when he dozed on the top deck of a London bus and the latter, years later also when dozing in front of a fire.

Otto Loewi who made the discovery that chemical substances are involved in triggering off nerve impulses to muscles actually received it in a dream.

Frederick Banting testified that three sentences communicated to him one night led to his discovery of insulin.

James Watt, in a flash of insight, received the ideas which produced the steam engine. He insisted he was not at all responsible. The ideas were given to him.

Brahams has openly said: "Spirit is Universal. It is the creative energy of the Cosmos. The soul of man is not conscious of its powers until it is enlightened by Spirit."

Max Burch, who composed that lovely violin 'Concerto' said: "My most beautiful melodies have come to me in dreams."

"From some alien energy the visions come." said Emerson. "I am trying to find out where matter ends and Spirit begins." Einstein said it emphatically and proudly when he was asked to comment on his work on the atom.

People who predict the future virtually establish the fact that there is a future. And because it is predictable, it is obviously already laid out and established, but within the framework of the broad future — life and death — there is plenty of roaming space for the free will. For quite manifestly, it is the way we respond to the expected and the unexpected. The disappointments and tragedies of life do determine our state of mind, not the actual event itself.

As a humorous illustration of this "roaming space" theory, Jesse Steran, who has made elaborate research on occultism, tells the story of how he had been visiting the fortune-tellers and psychics with an experimental subject, a young actress in her 20's. After the last visit, their taxi narrowly avoided a collision with a lorry by braking suddenly. The girl remonstrated in alarm with the driver. Jesse Steran reminded his companion daily that she should have no fear as the Seers had predicted she would live to be 85. "I know," was the reply, "but I don't want to spend the last 60 years of it in a plaster cast."

These are just a few examples but they all refer to the inspiration and help that came from "outside"/"the occult world"/ "the other world."

11

Colour Healing

Colour healing, like spiritual or psychic healing, is a perfectly scientific therapy through which almost every disease is treated efficaciously without any side effects. It has been practised since time immemorial. Effective use of colour healing was made in the Golden Age of Greece and in the Healing Temples of Light and Colour at Heliopolis in ancient Egypt and so also in China and India.

Roland Hunt, the author of *The Seven Keys to Colour Healing,* who has made astounding research on this scientific therapy says: "To regard Colour Healing for one moment, as anything less would be like the woman who recalled only that electricity was something that heated her press iron whereas we know it is a cosmic energy that man has learned to give artificial light, heat and cold, transport facilities and other services and comforts to the human family throughout the world. Colour, similarly offers its comforts and services to man, indeed, electrical and light (colour) waves have a common origin in the Sun Power — the great comforter and energiser."

The ancient Egyptians knew the potential power and influence of colour and in their temples (Karnak and Thebes) there were colour halls where research in the use of colour and colour healing was practised scientifically. Manuscripts are available from these early times which confirm that in India, China and Egypt every healer priest possessed complete systems of colour science based on the law of correspondence between the sevenfold nature of man and the seven-fold division of the solar spectrum.

In America, Professor Woods, Dr. C. S. Abbott and Ellis L. Manning, physicist of the General Electric Company, independently of each other, have produced motors running entirely by solar power. In colour healing, the white sunlight is used, in all its spectrum of colour wavelengths, to run the motor organs of the human machine efficiently — not only to restore the physical body, but also to tone up and refresh the mind and nourish the Spirit. The energy-waves from the sun create, sustain and renew life on our earth and on all other' planets in the zodiac, which in turn reflect their vibratory rays on each other. The self-same principles that sustain life in the cosmic system naturally sustain man in his lesser, microcosmic system, that is in the working of the major glandular organs of his body.

I would like to quote Roland Hunt again: "If through some failure in Cosmic Law and Order, the earth were to be plunged into complete and continued darkness for about a few weeks, and then restored to light, all vegetation would be found to have lost its colourful vitality, to have become anaemic, and would finally wither and disappear. There would correspondingly have been a similar effect on the health and vitality of humanity. We all depend on light more than is yet fully realised, for, as we see above, even our foods are densified chemical light-waves, and this we shall refer to more fully presently."

We have seen that people living in insufficiently lighted houses and so also those living in congested cities and towns suffer from a large variety of physical and nervous ailments—many of which originate in either mental or emotional perversion or inversion. These people are plagued with all manner of inhibitions. But people living in villages, bathing in plenty of rich sunlight and surrounded by plants and flowers (with essential colour vibrations) are healthier than their counterparts in congested cities. All in all, colour is undoubtedly an integral part of our lives. It brings us health, joy and gaiety and so also healing when required. Visible or otherwise it does affect us powerfully, for in it we live and have our being.

"Colour," says Hunt, "has the beautiful and purposeful mission of alleviating both classes of disease not with the patchwork substitutes of drugs, but with the pristine power of Light, which works on ALL levels of our being. Truly, it is very largely due to our general inability to illumine our lives emotionally, mentally and spiritually, that we have loss of tone, or disease physically."

It is thus the prolonged lack of nourishing light that brings about a light starvation in certain parts of the physical body, and impairs the circulation of life forces through that part resulting in a diseased organ.

As early as in 1880, Shri Jwala Prasad, Munsiff of Benares, said about himself: "In 1880 I was in search of something by which I could be of use to humanity at large. I had already become a tolerably fair magnetiser. This practice developed in me a general love for humanity and for the treatment of diseases. But I found that I could not attend to all patients, who kept on increasing. This system of treatment was not such as to prevail in the long run, and I was in search of humanity. At last I came to have *Babbitt's Health Manual* in which I found the principles of Chromopathy recorded, and I have been practising this science ever since. I am now in a position to state that this treatment is to supersede all other treatments. It is at once the cheapest, the mildest and the most effective of all treatments known. It is especially suited to all who are spiritually inclined and I hope every lover of mankind will try to spread its principles among the general public."

Modern research, physics and metaphysics, are today busy uncovering the wisdom and legacy of the ancient seers regarding the use of colour in healing. Doctors and scientists have interested themselves in research into the use of nature's finer forces, for the effective healing of many illnesses. They have actually been using colour therapeutically with astounding results. They are convinced that chromotherapy restores bodily imbalance through the application of beams of coloured light to the body. Robert Hunt's book *Researches on Light in its Chemical Relations* is an important treatise in which he describes the influences on plant growth of selected applications of light.

Dr. E.D. Babbitt has also published a monumental work describing the effects of the different colours of the spectrum and their use as healing agents. In 1933, Dr. D. P. Ghadiali, an Indian scientist who worked and taught in the U.S.A., discovered the scientific principles which explain why and how the different coloured rays have various definite therapeutic effects on the organism. His research for two decades has given us *The Spectra Chromometry Encyclopaedia*, a memorable and challenging book on colour therapy. According to his research the process of living in a healthy condition involves a proper balance within the body of all the colour energies. If this balance is disturbed or violated, disease follows.

The earth obtains a regular flow of energy from the sun's rays and all elements known on the earth are found in the sun. This is shown by spectroscopic analysis, which has a scientific basis. It is an indisputable fact that the sun's rays bring us the energies of every known element from which chemical combinations are made. The white light contains the energies of all elements and chemicals found in the sun and the sun pours white light energy all the time into the atmosphere charging it with various types of energy that is so essential to sustain life. Here are seven primary rays and seven centres in the body which predominantly attract these rays:

1. Red — The Base Centre:
   At the root of the spine correlating with coccygeal or gonad centre.
2. Orange — The Splenic Centre:
   In the small of the back.
3. Yellow — The Solar Plexus Centre:
   In the centre of the back.

4. Green	—	The Heart Centre: In line with the heart between the shoulder blades.
5. Blue	—	The Throat Centre: At the base of the skull.
6. Indigo	—	The Pineal Gland Centre: In the centre of the forehead.
7. Violet	—	The Pituitary Centre: In the dome of the head.

There are seven Power Centres (these are also known as Chakras or Power Wheels), each under a particular colour creating a pattern on which the physic is built. The seven Power Centres link with the spinal cord at definite intervals. In the human being energy is drawn in through the Power Centres and distributed over the whole body.

The Red and the Orange Power Centres influence the physical and etheric level in man and supply most vital energies required by the body. The Yellow Power Centre influences the lower mental level. It also has to do with emotional influences. The Green Power Centre governs the higher mind and also influences the higher emotions such as sympathy, compassion and understanding. The Blue Power Centre is the Centre of spiritual elements. The Blue, Red and Yellow Power Centres collectively influence and build up harmony for physical and mental health.

12

Psychic Surgery

Psychic surgery, like psychic healing, has a definite place in psychic phenomena. Thousands of bodies have been opened with bare hands and without the use of anaesthesia by the psychic surgeons. Many patients have been completely cured although this particular surgery has no place in modern medical books!

It is indeed a poor reflection on orthodox medicine that sufferers — particularly women and children — in their thousands flock to Manila and Brazil in a desperate effort to obtain cures, and this they do in full measure. The phenomena of a human body being opened with bare hands, tissues removed with human blood flowing, quick and easy closure of the opening without trace, have gripped people's imagination throughout the world today.

Doctors who have witnessed these operations are no doubt completely baffled. They have no logical explanation to give for phenomena that have no place in medical science. Removal of rusty fish hooks, pebbles, broken glass, stones, cysts, tumours and other objects by psychic force is so much numbo-jumbo to the critical clinical mind!

According to sceptics the phenomena of the body being opened with bare hands and quick closure of the body without trace could be due to hypnotism. But how can one go on about hypnotising a camera that has recorded thousands of feet of operations in colour? The world has yet to produce a magician who can materialise objects in broad daylight under the close scruitiny of a slow motion picture. The Divine Power Research Society of India headed by Dr. K. K. Datey, an eminent doctor, told newsmen in Bombay that the society planned to invite psychic surgeons from the Philippines where this form of surgery is quite popular, to demonstrate their skill, believed to be partly 'Divine'. Dr. Datey said, if psychic surgery could dispense with long periods of hospitalisation, absence from work and expenses of conventional operations (which are huge indeed), it could do good service to humanity. It has done, indeed. Dr. Datey, who was one of the few senior-most 'giants' in the medical profession, was bold enough to speak on psychic surgery, which, according to many in the profession, is mere hallucination. Dr. Ramchandra Bhonsle has shown excitingly successful results in psychic surgery in his Rooms in Bombay. Distinguished persons treated by Dr. Bhonsle include Pandit Jawaharlal Nehru, Lord Mountbatten. Dr. Rajendra Prasad, Lal Bahadur Shastri, and a number of other living personalities, who are equally distinguished. It is time orthodox medical prejudice is banished. It is time more and more members of the medical profession examined the psychic surgeons under their own conditions. If they bring open minds to bear and show willingness to obey psychic laws, I am sure medical history will be made.

John G. Fuller in his book, *Arigo: Surgeon of the Rusty Knife*, has this to say: "The work of no other so-called psychic surgeon has ever been documented as thoroughly as that of Arigo. Arigo was unique: no proof of fraud has ever been uncovered. How he did what he apparently did remains a mystery, concerning which the reader will have to make his own judgement."

Born on October 18, 1918, his formal name of Jose Pedro de Freitas was dropped in favour of Arigo. He claimed to be 'possessed' by a team of spirit doctors and surgeons, particularly by a German doctor called Adolpho Fritz who did the operations and dictated the prescriptions through Arigo.

Dr. Henry Andrija K. Puharich, with a medical degree from North Western University and a keen interest in psychic phenomena, went all the way to Brazil with a team of well-known physicians to collect evidence, see for himself Arigo's operations and have the healings attested by other local doctors. Dr. Henry Puharich saw Arigo placing his patients one by one against a wall and driving his knife into a tumour or a cyst, an eye or an ear, and remove unwanted growths without anaesthesia, hypnotic suggestion, or antiseptics. Bleeding amounted to little more than a trickle.

Arigo practised surgery and brought about innumerable cures and yet the Regional Council of Medicine of the Brazilian State of Miniais Gerais and the Roman Catholic Church brought a court action against Arigo and arrested him in order to stop his 'illegal' practice! However, the Brazilian Senator, Senhor Lutio Bittincourt who suffered from lung cancer declared incurable by a team of doctors, was operated upon by Jose Arigo, in trance and cured completely. Jose Arigo was thus saved from the jail sentence. Being not only impressed but also thoroughly convinced, Dr. Puharich decided to get a benign lipoma (tumour) on the inside of his right elbow operated upon by Arigo. In less than ten seconds Arigo removed the lipoma with his 'unsterilised fingers and knife', from a slit of half an inch made with a penknife with a bare trickle of blood dripping down from it. Two days later, the incision was completely closed even without the help of any sutures. The lipoma was sent for pathological investigation to rule out any doubt about its being a sleight of hand. Dr. Puharich had this particular operation filmed by his own cameramen. A number of other operations were also filmed by the cameramen.

According to the most scrupulous findings, it is a fact that among the thousands of his patients who have attested to his ability, there were doctors, radiologists, pathologists, actors, statesmen, lawyers, politicians from many countries and leading scientists.

Dr. Robert Laidlow, former Director of Psychiatry at the Roosevelt Hospital, screened the colour films of Arigo's surgery a number of times to convince many a scientist that Arigo's operations were beyond the skill of even the most highly trained and experienced surgeons. Senhor Arthur da Costa E. Silva, the Brazilian President, went to the extent of promising his personal support to Arigo in order to build a spacious hospital where Arigo could attend to the unending queues of patients coming for his Divine surgery.

Eyewitness reports of 'Miracles' of psychic surgery performed in trance by Arigo are also published by America's ace investigator Joseph Hansell in *Cosmic Star*. He described his visit to the healer's campo in the village of Congonhas do Campo as the "commanding highlight" of an extensive research tour amongst Brazil's more than ten million spiritualists.

"I have never witnessed such dedication anywhere, as I did the day I observed this man. Sick folk queue up daily to see Arigo. Some are carried in on stretchers, some in wheel chairs, some in great pain, and some have been waiting for days to see this man. We saw the street filled with the sick, the lame and the blind."

Arigo was investigated by a group of 60 outstanding doctors, professors and scientists of the University of Sao Paulo who also invited him to their University to demonstrate.

Joseph Hansell adds: "The day my wife and I visited him, I witnessed what I also considered to be miracles. Healing miracles are also brought through Arigo's healing prayers. He has turned down some patients' requests because he says their mission is finished here on earth, and it would be wrong for him to pray for them and hold them in the physical world."

Arigo died in January 1971 of coronary thrombosis. Flags flew at half mast with two days of mourning throughout Brazil as more than twenty-thousand patients watched the body interred!

Every Wall a Door is an interesting paperback written by a famous reporter from the U.S.A., Anne Dooley. It is a gripping and dramatic account of surgery by the Brazilian Healer, Lourival de Freitas. Her lung condition, diagnosed by doctors as inoperable twenty years earlier, was cured. The surgery was filmed and pictoral evidence of it is included in the paperback. According to die author, Lourival de Freitas inserted scissors into her mouth prior to removing her tonsils followed by the removal of coagulated blood clot from her back and stitching the incision. Before her operation Anne underwent twice daily postural drainage. During surgery she ejected blood-stained mucus and a large clot. After ten days she felt fully recovered. She testified that the tissue ejected orally and the blood clot were not surreptitiously smuggled in from any butcher's shop!

Robert Copley (75) of St. Ives, Huntingdon, Cambs, an eminent lawyer, trained by his professional work to assess evidence, has presented his account of cures by psychic surgery he witnessed in the Philippines. I had the unique pleasure of meeting this man. He witnessed more than 250 of these spirit operations and took colour films of 25 treatments. The learned lawyer does not disguise his wholehearted admiration of the Philippine surgeons who he calls 'these wonderful people of God'. His solicitor colleagues know of his extensively documented work on the surgeons. He says: "The one disease no one seems able to heal is dogmatic stupidity." It seems logical to suppose that the same or similar laws are in use in both the Philippines and Brazil. I think I am correct in saying that these operations cannot be weighed in the balance of medical laws so far as they are practised today. Cold, hard, clinical appraisement is like water on a fire. Psychic laws must be given their own position and value in the search for truth. When these phenomena are under scrutiny, these laws must be obeyed. Medical knowledge must, so to speak, be by-passed. By the use of these psychic laws, hygiene is completely ignored. Investigators cannot find any case of infection caused by psychic surgery. Pain is completely controlled without drugs. No scars remain visible even after many operations. The speed has to be seen to be appreciated. For example: "Jose Mercado attended 451 patients from 11 a.m. one Saturday to Sunday evening. I have seen operations on people standing sitting or lying, take place in seconds." Robert Copley told the world all this through his sensational article published in the Psychic News of London. It was scepticism about "miracle cures" in the Philippines that made him decide to see for himself. He tells of successful operations performed on him and his wife. The four famous surgeons whose operations with astounding results have been witnessed by the most scrupulous critics are: Romy Bularin, Jose Mercado, Juan Blanche and Josephina Sison

Carl Lahmann, the Australian author from Auchen-flower, Brisbane, and his wife Shirley made three fact-finding visits to the Philippines. He is also a famous spirit healer and has cured many "incurable" patients with the help of his spirit doctors, for more than 20 years. He has helped a number of physicians and surgeons with his "intuitive diagnosis" for which Harry Edwards was famous internationally. "We went with open minds and are convinced the power to part with matter is a genuine gift," says Lehmann in his latest report after his third fact-finding visit to the Philippines.

There are innumerable people in our country — some of whom I know personally — who have undergone psychic surgery and have been cured completely. Yet, there is not a single patient who is bold enough to admit the cure through psychic surgery (or through psychic healing!) It is difficult to know why truth is concealed. Probably it is due to certain complexes and prejudices. On the other hand, Tony Roche, the internationally known sportsman, was at once willing to tell the world as loudly as he could that had it not been for the two operations he underwent in the Philippines for his arm injury and Achilles' tendon, he could not have fought his way back to the top of the game (*The Illustrated Weekly of India*, July 27, 1975).

13

Cases Healed: Some Revealing Comments

A young person of thirty-two who had seldom suffered from any disease, woke up one morning with acute pain in the stomach and with his left hand and leg almost paralysed. He was unable to speak. Those who brought him to me assured me that this young man was neither an alcoholic nor irregular in his way of living. As he was placed on my couch for examination, my hand developed a peculiar trembling vibration. Incidentally, since 1968, these strange vibrations in my fingers have become a constant feature. While examining this young man, I found that my hand automatically went to his stomach where I felt an unhealthy lump. The word "malignancy" burst out from my lips! Subsequently it was found that the hospital surgeon had come to the same conclusion after a biopsy test. Thus my intuitive diagnosis was confirmed medically!

Fortunately I was also able to heal the patient who is still alive and free from all pain and discomfort. The surgeon who had done no more than just examine this man takes the full credit for his recovery. Does a mere biopsy test imply any treatment, and can it always cure malignancy?

In this connection Harry Edwards writes in his book, *The Power of Spiritual Healing*, thus: "Very accurate diagnosis is received by experienced healers intuitively. This can be understood when it is recalled that the actual diagnosis in healing is determined by the spirit doctors.

"That this is a fact is proved by the authenticity of the healings themselves, for, in order to produce a given effect in any material sense, there must be an intelligently applied force to bring about the change. So when a healer is in a condition of attunement with both the patient and the spirit doctor, the latter is able to convey intuitively the diagnosis of the case and can counsel how to assist in overcoming th symptoms of the trouble."

Edwards further says: "In Contact Healing diagnosis is often received through the healer's hand, and the method by which this is experienced will vary with different healers. There is, however, an effect which is commonly felt by healer and patient alike, and that is that when the healer's hand covers the affected area, both are conscious of a sensation of penetrating heat flowing from the hand into the patient's body —sometimes the opposite is felt — a sensation of intense cold. As the hands move away from the affected part, the sensation of heat or cold vanishes, returning as soon as the hand reverts to that particular area. By these means, a healer is able to correctly diagnose the site of the trouble. It is interesting to note that though the healer and the patient may feel the heat, if a thermometer is placed between the hand and the patient the thermometer does not register the temperature or the heat."

My Guide not only helped me in cases of actual contact healing, but also helped me in healing patients residing in far away places of the country. These were also treated successfully in absentia with the help of my Guide at a particular hour each day. I kept a monthly record of these patients and was gratified to note the improvement in their condition. I would not however claim that every patient was healed. Such a claim would be false and therefore unethical. But many patients from the western countries and the Middle East have been cured. So far, out of about 16,400 patients, about 67 per cent have been cured in absent healing. I feel that this is a fairly good percentage.

To some extent the healing percentage is even more than what we find in medical records. I would like to make here one important observation that the rate of cure is as high as 67 per cent despite the fact that patients go in for spiritual healing as a last resort — that is when the medical profession has given up as incurable those chronic cases which are very difficult. In spite of this if the proportion of spiritual healing is as high as 67 per cent as is indicated by the systematic data maintained through the years, it is something to be proud of. Healers all over the world have made it clear that taking appropriate medical treatment side by side with spiritual healing is not ruled out. Since healing is concerned with only the spirit body, the physical body may well be left to the care of the medical profession. As a matter of fact, when spiritual healing and medical therapy are combined, the results are sometimes remarkable. It being a two-pronged attack on the disease, the results are often better and lasting. Unfortunately, in India today, there is quite a lot of prejudice against spiritual or psychic healing, which is a great pity since our people can scarcely afford modern medical treatment. Moreover, spiritual or psychic healing had its origin in India which undoubtedly has a rich spiritual and religious heritage.

It is indeed very sad that this progressive art of healing is rejected in a country of spiritual traditions, whereas in the western countries, in Brazil, Africa, Australia, and the Philippines this art-cum-science has assumed great importance and healing centres and sanctuaries have been organised to give refuge and relief to hundreds of sufferers. Even Russia has been spending huge sums of money on research work in psychic healing, producing healers of remarkable calibre and repute. As a matter of fact, in European countries, healing is openly practised in hospitals along with medical therapy, producing fantastic cures. The journalists abroad are open-minded and they go out of their way to contact healers, collect data of the successful application of healing and then give prominent coverage to these reports. Should not Indian journalists and medical authorities emulate this healthy and scientific approach of their foreign colleagues?

Reverting to my healing work —in the sphere of contact healing, I am happy to mention an unusually successful case of a medical man who was passing thirty to forty watery stools a day with blood and mucus. The patient did not feel better despite massive does of antibiotics and anti-amoebic treatment. In five days this man was reduced to skin and bones in which condition he was brought to my rooms on a stretcher. I gave one sitting of contact healing and, as he left, I confess I had doubts about his recovery. "How can he survive?"—this was the nagging fear in my mind. Little did I expect that this case would be entered in my files as a very important and a remarkable one. I recalled Harry Edwards's instant healing successes! The same night my patient rang me up to report about his sudden and incredible recovery. I was amazed and full of gratitude to God.

A similar case of a girl aged eight years, which was given up by the doctors, was treated by me a little later. The stools could not be stopped for more than a fortnight, but the bleeding stopped so that the child was pronounced out of danger. There is one question that is persistently put to me: "Do doctors come to you?" "Do doctors refer their patients to you?" The answer to both these questions is an emphatic "Yes". I have in my records cases of several doctors as well as their patients coming to me to be treated, and though they recover, it must be regretfully said that these persons like to keep it a secret for reasons that are too obvious. In my opinion it is selfish and arrogant to reap the benefits of a cure through a spiritual healer and then fight shy of giving credit where credit is due. Painful as such attitude is, a healer must not allow himself to be disturbed by these considerations, lest it interfere with his peace of mind and affect his work.

I would like to report one particular case of healing of a hospital nurse who was referred to me by a noted surgeon. The patient suffered from asthma for well over fourteen years. Massive doses of cortisone had left baneful marks on her mind and body. The patient was treated with contact healing over a period of eight months. She was given complete freedom from a disease which had made her life miserable. The doctors, however, did not hesitate to attribute her cure to the medical treatment she had received over the years. But the patient knew only too well what had cured her, and she had the courage to admit this in her letter to me.

As I have said earlier, patients come for healing either too late or when a cure through any other conventional therapy is absolutely ruled out. Horace Leaf has most aptly declared about this peculiar attitude of most of the patients: "One of the drawbacks from which spiritual healing suffers is an inner scepticism of those who come to the healers with negative thoughts." These patients come to healers as a last resort because there is no other hope. Many healers notice the cynical attitude of such patients. There is a kind of "I bet you cannot cure me" look on their faces.

I have a letter from a girl of 22 who came with a history of epileptic fits. The girl's parents were naturally very upset, knowing too well that with such a disease, there would be no hope of the girl being able to settle down in marriage. I administered two contact healing treatments before the girl went back to Assam. Subsequently I was happy to hear that not only the epileptic fits became shorter in duration, but that the fits recurred at longer and longer intervals until after a few months the girl was completely rid of them. The recovery ot this patient did not surprise me because her letters apprised me of her intimate connection with my Guide. It seems that at a particular time in the morning this girl would feel the fragrance of tube roses which are my Guide's favourite flowers. The girl also saw frequently an orange-coloured flame. In the very special Seance arranged by me, I was told that, in fact, my Guide was present with the girl with tube roses and a torch.

The case of another girl from Delhi is also noteworthy. This girl had a patch of Leucoderma on her neck which caused her great agony. She sent me a photograph of herself showing the spot on the neck. She begged me to heal her. It took some time for the disease to come under control. When this happens many patients are apt to become impatient and displeased and lose faith. However, my faith in my Guide remained unshaken and I was very soon rewarded with the news of the girl's complete recovery, and also the news of her marriage to which the grateful father sent me an invitation!

Equally remarkable is the case of a person suffering from acute arthritis which prevented him from walking as the knees had pronounced swelling. Absent healing was started immediately. In the beginning the monthly reports of this case were not encouraging for about three months. After that came the amazing news that the patient felt that he was given an injection on the afflicted area in his sleep. The patient actually detected the prick-marks of injections on both his knees. Thus an unseen power healed this patient and a month later he could walk normally and without pain.

Two Cases of Malignancy Healed

A very serious case of malignancy in the liver was referred to me by a friend in Calcutta. The lady so afflicted, 32 years old, lay in the hospital with unbearable pain. The doctors had to give her an injection every two hours to relieve the pain. Absent treatment was started by me and within a week the patient was absolutely free from pain and enjoyed all the comfort she longed for. However, the patient died after 46 days. Surprisingly enough the members of the family were grateful to me because they knew that the end at least was free from pain and torture and the lady was peaceful before she died. The family attributed this blessing to spiritual healing. Death is inevitable when one's life span is finished. It may be mentioned, however, that the patient was referred to me rather too late, for the disease had spread to all her vital organs.

There was another case of malignancy I treated of a young woman of 32 who had a persistently oozing boil in her left breast. Advanced cancer was diagnosed. The surgeon wanted to remove the entire breast though he felt that the patient could not survive for more than two months. The young woman refused to go in for surgery and came to me for spiritual healing. Within a month of contact healing there was considerable improvement. The pain and the oozing stopped completely after six months and the girl was healed. After enjoying a normal and a happy life for two years, the girl met with a serious accident and death was instantaneous. My Guide comforted me by saying that the cancer was completely cured but life and death are in the hands of the Almighty. I should not therefore feel frustrated because, after all, as the patient's husband also admitted, death is inevitable when one's time is up. But the husband was grateful that his wife enjoyed comfort and happiness for two and a half years before she died.

In concluding this chapter, I would once again like to state that to get the maximum benefit from a spiritual healer, it is necessary to cultivate the virtues of Patience and Faith.

14

Loknayak Jayaprakash Narayan: My Ideal Patient

I am singularly happy and particularly privileged and honoured to mention one name — a person whose tremendous contribution not only to India at the national level, but also to the social and spiritual uplift of humanity at large is recognized by one and all. His name is Loknayak Jayaprakash Narayan. It was my good fortune to treat him for four years. Towards the end of 1975, when he was taken seriously ill, I was approached by four very close friends of J.P. who sought my help. All these friends have chosen to remain anonymous to this date. It was indeed a difficult task for me to go to the Jaslok Hospital to meet J.P. and much more so to treat him. I was not supposed to break the hospital rules because J.P. was looked after by a team of expert doctors. Somehow the people who had approached me made it possible for me to see J.P. at the Jaslok Hospital and accordingly psychic healing was administered from the day I saw him. (I had met him earlier in 1971, when he was introduced to me by a common friend, Mr. Govardhandas Ruparel, and once again at the cremation ground when Mr. Ruparel passed away and J.P. had specially come to Bombay to attend his funeral. We had quite some time to talk on Psychic Healing.)

Besides being receptive, J.P. showed signs of early recovery even when he was subsequently treated in absentia. I had taken maximum care to be totally out of the picture as far as J.P.'s treatment was concerned, because I did not care for publicity. I was more concerned about this man's recovery rather than fame. The results were very encouraging and the healing intercessions were dropped by the first half of 1977 when J.P. seemed well enough to go about his business as normally as any healthy person, except for the dialysis which was necessary for him due to the damaged kidney. But in spite of the dialysis, J.P. did lead a normal and an active life. In fact when a physician went to Patna to examine him in November, 1978, he was surprised about the miraculous improvement in J.P.'s health. The physician admitted that J.P. was perhaps the only person in the world at that age who was so comfortable in spite of dialysis. According to the personal letter of J.P.'s secretary to me, the physician was honest enough to acknowledge that it was something other than medical treatment that kept J.P. alive and as active as he was then. However, in early 1979 there was a relapse in J.P.'s health and he started passing blood in his stools. It was then that several persons including the earlier friends approached me for immediate help. This time however my meeting J.P. was difficult because the doctors attending on him were very strict, most uncooperative and did not wish an outsider to go near J.P. although J.P. himself did wish to see me. So did his private secretary. Hospital rules could not be broken and hence I preferred to see J.P. once without anyone's knowledge, as a visitor and could do whatever little I could through a hurried, 'illegal' (!) intercession. This was after he was brought back from the United States of America. People all over the world were anxious about him and the press issued fluctuating bulletins about his health. At this time, I thought it necessary to call on J.P. personally and I managed to do it with the help of his P. A., Mr. Thomas Abraham. I know I was breaking the hospital rules but I could not help doing it because I cared for J.P.'s health much more than I cared for the unreasonable rules made by some with vested interests.

The meeting was very effective. There was definite progress in his health and, except for his weakness, there were no serious complications. Letters started pouring in thanking me for all that I was doing for J.P. through absent healing. Although I have never taken credit for J.P.'s cure and his return journey to Patna safely, as per his wish, I did and do feel extremely happy that healing could do much, much more than anything in the world to keep that man alive and mentally alert till the day he passed away. I should emphatically state here that J.P.'s passing away was very peaceful. It was free from pain. He 'died' in his sleep. This is a peculiarity of patients who are treated the psychic way. One has to pass away some time and yet healing makes the passing peaceful.

Treating J.P. was all my pleasure and he was not under my obligation whatsoever. The only request I made him was to answer a few questions. He could dictate his answers to a few of them to his Secretary, Sachidanand. Unfortunately for me, Jayaprakashji passed away before he could take up the remaining questions to answer: Here are the questions and the answers:

Q. As per Shri Sachidanand's letter of the 15 December 1978, Dr. M. K. Mani, who visited you about a month ago, found you in fairly good condition. According to the doctor there was perhaps no patient in the world of your age living on dialysis today. He also feels that there is something beyond science that has sustained you so far. On this basis, do you feel that there are paranormal, i.e., para-physical and para-psychological forces working on man?

A. I believe there is some force that influences the destiny of man. I do not know how to describe it. You may call it para-physical or a spiritual force or give it some other name.

Q. There are 3,000 spiritual healers in the U.K. *The Journal of National Federation of Spiritual Healers and International Fellowship of Healing* has published three interviews — one of them with a leading physicist —on spiritual healing. On the lines of these interviews, our views are conditioned by science (mainly physical science) but there is tremendous time lag and present beliefs are based on earlier physics when physics has progressed towards more integral views of our world of material and para-material components. On this basis, we should move towards a holistic view of physical, psychological and spiritual covergence for health as well as living in general. Would you broadly agree with this view?

A. I have not given much thought to these matters. I however feel that a comprehensive view of life is necessary. Man is not only his physical self. Mind and Spirit are also important parts of his personality. The three interact and influence each other.

Q. The Author of *Uncertainty Principle*, Prof. Heisenberg states: "The concept of complementarity is meant to describe a situation in which we can look at one and the same event through two different frames of reference. These two frames actually exclude each other, but they also complement each other. Only the juxtaposition of these contradictory frames provides an exhaustive view of die appearances of the phenomena. Complementarity accords very neatly with the Cartesian dualism of matter and mind."

If matter and mind are complementary, a frame of reference suited only to the observation of matter cannot deal with problems of mind and/or Spirit. Similarly, a study of merely physical relationship by physical methods cannot enlighten us regarding psychic or spiritual phenomena.

What would be your views on this, please?

A. Matter, mind and spirit are parts of a single whole, and they must necessarily be complementary for a balanced growth of man.

Q. Illness can get a person in three ways, viz., through (a) body, (b) mind, or (c) soul. These all interact. For example, a bodily illness creates mental depression or mental illness rips spiritual values to shreds. If there are three ways for illness to attack, there can be three ways for the counterattack too: doctors through the body, psychiatrists through the mind, and spiritual or religious healers through the soul. What would be your views, please?

A. There can hardly be two opinions on the desirability of a three-pronged attack on any illness.

Q. Harry Edwards of the U.K. gave the Home Ministry and the British Medical Council a record of more than 1,300 medical cases of incurable cancer. He also has recorded miraculous cure of people who were lame, blind and invalid (cured before vast gatherings of people including doctors and journalists) with names, dates, photographs and authentic medical records of the U.K. doctors and institutions. Would it be (a) scientific and (b) reasonable to reject this evidence just because we cannot explain it?

A. It is not necessary to reject what cannot be explained. But the modern critical mind will not accept anything blindly. Evidence must be backed by reason, so as to be convincing enough to secure acceptance.

I wish J.P. had answered all the questions. There was no time; he had to go for more progressive work in response to His call.

15

My Encounter with Dilip Kumar Roy

I would like to mention yet another patient who received my contact and absent healing for his arthritis. He was Dada Dilip Kumar Roy. He was not only an author of international repute but has also been regarded as a cultural leader of the Artistic Renaissance in India. He was always ready to share generously with others his spiritual treasures — either through his eighty and more books or through his personal contact. He was a great conversationalist. He had intimate contacts and friendship with a galaxy of world's greatest men: Romain Rolland, Bertrand Russell, Dr. Sarvepalli Radhakrishnan, Gurudev Rabindranath Tagore, Mahatma Gandhi, Subhas Chandra Bose, Deshbandhu C. R. Das, Aldous Huxley, Pandit Jawaharlal Nehru, Maulana Abul Kalam Azad, Krishnaprem, Swami Ratndas and many, many others. He was a disciple of the world's highly respected seer: Shri Aurobindo Ghosh.

Meeting Dada Dilip Kumar Roy was an obsession with mo since I was a boy because he was one amongst the great and I was lucky and privileged to have had several communications with him and two personal, face to face, meetings.

It was in September 1978 that I first met him. His disciple, Shri Yogendra Rastogi, fixed up an appointment for me at Surya Apartments, Bhulabhai Desai Road, Bombay. The purpose of my visit was to examine him medically because he was ailing and give him medical advice and psychic healing intercessions in which he had great faith.

Unlike as in the case of Loknayak J.P., there were no obstacles in my way. There were no political leaders around trying to project themselves before the press and the TV cameras. There were neither any opportunists nor sycophants —no rules made with selfish motives and no super specialists trying to take the credit for his comfort or cure. I reached the Surya Apartments in time.

As the door opened, I felt as if I were in the holiest of holy places with an irresistible smell of incense spreading all around. Before I could go over to Dadaji's chamber, I felt the presence of astounding vibrations emanating from a room to the right where I saw one of the most beautiful idols of Lord Krishna with His flute, leaning against His Cow. The Puja Room, though not a temple, was charged with more vibrations and serenity than many a place of worship I have visited. I was led to his chamber where, seated on a sofa, were two great souls: Dada Roy and his daughter-disciple Indira Devi. Dadaji looked almost like a saint and had the voice of one. Clad in a pleasant, saffron coloured attire which suited him every inch, his piercing, beautiful brown eyes which seemed to speak, and a rich, white flowing beard, Dadaji bore a majestic personality. I was there before an extremely fair, charming spiritual genius who blessed me and listened to my medical advice as obediently as any meek patient would do. More than the medical treatment, Dadaji needed psychic healing which I gave him in full measure.

The healing power was instantaneous and flowed out without any effort or strain on my body — a tribute to that Saintly Soul. There was no occasion or time to speak to him on any subject as he was ailing. However, he said emphatically "I believe in psychic healing. I am too old now with a lot of complications: arthritis, bronchitis, a weak heart and hard hearing. But I know I will feel better." And he did feel better in course of time. He was kind enough to follow this up promptly through letters with his beautiful poetic language which was a joy to read. A friendly bond was thus established and, I know, my meeting was part of a Divine plan.

I went to see him again on November 25, 1978. He was at the typewriter as busy as ever despite his pains and aches. However, he was in a better mood to talk about many other things. It was in this meeting that I received a significant amount of knowledge and advice from him and I instinctively decided to accept him as my spiritual and intellectual guide. He repeated, "I do believe in psychic healing and so also psychic phenomena. I have seen miracles happening before me. I have seen the incurables cured with the healing touch." He showed me a number of coloured photographs in support of his statement, explaining to me in detail, each one of them. He did feel the necessity of propagating the authenticity of healing — specially the scientific aspect of it.

He invited me to Pune so that we could be together for more and longer time to discuss psychic healing and other phenomena. That day he had a gift for me—one I shall ever cherish as the most precious possession of my life, *Wings and Bonds*— his latest book dealing with the Soul's evolution through the vicissitudes of its eternal God-quest, opposed by the earth-pull of lesser loves. The drama is enacted on the stage of life sponsored by the Unattainable and counteracted by the senses' nostalgic cravings for little pleasures, endorsed by reason's approval and scepticism's addiction to Realism. The book was rendered more precious by his autograph.

Dr. R.K. Keni

You have come in love
To cure me with your art I welcome you kind friend
With all my heart
With my love and blessing 5th November, 1978.

Dada Dilip Kumar Roy

"Dear Dr. Keni,

I am sorry I could not reply to your kind letter last week. My birthday was responsible. A good many friends came to wish me a long life. But believe me, I have deeply appreciated your courtesy and genuine solicitude. May the Lord make you His agent for hoaling people. I thank you once more for your loving kindness. May the Lord bless you all the time.

With my best wishes and affectionate blessing, I remain,

26th January, 1979. Yours cordially,

Dada Dilip Kumar Roy"

I have yet to meet a more dignified, a more sincere, a more compassionate, vibrant and versatile man full of humility in spite of all his greatness — a great soul whose presence I still feel along with the irresistible smell of the incense, all the time. Dada Dilip Kumar Roy passed away peacefully on January 6, 1980.

16

Healing of a Saint

Dr. Basantlal Malhotra, who is both a patient and a very close and dear friend of mine in Bombay, brought me word that Swami Muktanandji of Ganeshpuri desired to see me. It was as incredible as Sathya Sai Baba inviting me. There are thousands of Swami Muktanandji's admirers and disciples who are dying to have his "Darshan" which is sc difficult to get. Should I not have therefore felt gratified on being asked to see him? I was all the more excited when 1 knew that I would have to examine him as he had a weal; heart and subsequently heal him. Already he was seen by a team of cardiologists and he was under their treatment But Baba Muktanandji thought healing would be better for him.

This meeting was very much a part of the Divine plan mentioned earlier. I knew that my Healing Guides were with me all the time when I reached the place because on my arrival with Dr. Malhotra and his wife Vidya, I was not only ushered in by one of his attendants without having to wait even for a minute, but I was invited by Baba to sit on a chair next to him while his disciples, who comprised important people from all walks of life, squatted on the floor in front of Baba. Muktanandji was relaxed and welcomed me as if I were his bosom friend. He narrated a number of anecdotes and his personal experiences to me and the others before I could examine him. Words flowed from him with great ease. There was a Divine touch in his voice. There was also a tremendous appeal in his narration. He took his own time to give me complete relaxation and make me feel at home. He thereafter subjected himself to my medical check-up. His heart was weak. He had breathlessness and yet he was not at all bothered about his trouble. He was charged with Divine energy and he surrendered himself to God.

When I wished to heal him he was at once ready and greatly interested. I could very freely administer contact healing in the presence of all his disciples who had gathered there for his Darshan. There was a radiant smile on Baba's lips. His face shone radiantly with his eyes closed, he was in deep meditation — a Saintly Baba linked with God! He told me he felt much better after the healing intercession but he wished to give me some of his own healing energy. This he did by breathing into my mouth several times. His breath was charged with immense heat which I could not bear and yet could not resist because I felt mentally much better and in a short while increasingly healthy every moment. Baba advised me not to continue my work at the Bombay Hospital for a week until I had absorbed all the healing power he had breathed into me. Baba then ordered distribution of very special sweets and pushing a big piece into my mouth he prayed silently for my health and progress in healing and medical work. Believe me, there has been tremendous progress in my healing capacity since then. It is difficult to come across in life such saintly persons with such a large number of disciples —such humble souls, so kind, so great, so godly. I am proud because he fed me with his own hands. I am proud because he gave me, so much of his healing power and energy which I still feel in my body and in my fingers.

I shall cherish his contact all through my life. He still receives my absent healing and he knows well that he receives it.

17

Eminent Journalists confirm the Power of Psychic Healing

Mrs. Indrani Dutta Gupta, who is one of the most brilliant journalists I have met, was one of my patients. She has written a number of articles on psychic healing in important publications, in English as well as in Bengali. I reproduce below a part of one of her articles published in the *Sunday Amrit Bazar Patrika* of Calcutta dated 25 December 1977:

> 'Preach the gospel and heal the sick', Christ had commanded men. Indeed, all saints and genuine preachers are known for their considerable healing abilities. Above them are men who heal but do not usually preach — the professional medical men. Many of them are ardent devotees of their God or Deity and believe that regular prayers help them diagnose and treat patients well.

"During this century, a distinctly non-medical form of healing has gained popularity in the West and this is spiritual healing which may continue side by side with medical treatment. It is a definite revival or popularisation of what has been at the basis of all healing from time immemorial — the banking on powers as yet unharnessed by man and by supplication to them. Spiritual healing has never gone out of India, where for lack of good medical facilities people in remote villages are compelled to turn to spiritualism, often through occultists. But it seems that the Western type of spiritual healing, often termed 'Faith Healing' or 'Psychic Healing', is developing into a futuristic medicine and is making an inroad into India. This involves not only prayers to a

Universal, Omnipotent God — direct or through Christ, or through a Saint or a family Deity — but also a friendship between a healer and at least one soul who has passed away. The friendship may be established through planchettes or other forms of Seances.

"The Science behind this is what any Yogi will teach: that a disease need not always enter through the physical body alone. Often, the weak mind of the patient, his inner panic for instance, may be to blame, as also some imbalance deeper down inside his psyche, or his soul, or his spirit, due either to inherited conditions outside him or the imbalance may also be due to bad habits, lack of will power and finally, Karma —. in this life and in the previous ones. Karma is a Universal concept and not merely a Hindu one: in Revelation, 22, 12 Jesus Christ has promised 'to give every man according as his work shall be'.

"Spiritual Healing tries to cure a sickness — physical or mental — with the help of spirit doctors, however implausible it may appear to be. These spirits can often go into the deepest roots of ill health and remove the causes, if only we are receptive to the work they are ever ready to do for us. They find it easier to work on religious people, because genuine heart-felt prayers from the patient and his family to their God, is an immense help. It is also not very difficult to help heal die truly open-minded man, even if he is initially sceptical. It is more difficult to penetrate into the innermost being of the man who is determined not to believe in spiritual forces, or to heal the person who has no will to recover.

"Apart from the Ashrams and hermitages, there are spiritual healing centres all over the Western world now. Healers work under churches, in hospitals and on their own, under inspiration from God or Spirit Guides. Many of us are familiar with the story of Arigo: Surgeon of the Rusty Knife (John Fuller, Reader's Digest Book Choice, May 1975). but few know that research has been started on these apparently unscientific and freakish modes of healing in Universities like Stanford. Benevolent work through spirit help may become scientifically accepted soon.

"Spiritual healers are very sensitive persons, with an inborn urge to heal that helps them feel for the patient. Without this emotive response, kept under check from outward view, even a doctor cannot be successful.

"Perhaps the most famous of modem spiritual healers in the West is the late Harry Edwards who founded the Spiritual Healing Sanctuary at Burrows Lea, Shere, Guildford, Surrey, England. Harry Edwards was guided by the spirit of Lister from the other world as Dr. Fritz guided Arigo. He had cured millions, with the help of aids from both worlds either by the touch of his fingers (contact healing) or by prayers (absent healing). And he still continues helping healers from the other world. Anyone from any part of die world can write to this Sanctuary for assistance. Incurable cases like arthritis, deafness, blindness, asthma and other chronic problems are regularly cured by Spirit Healers although cure cannot be guaranteed, because of Karmic limitations and other factors. A Spirit Healer is generally an altruistic soul, purer at heart than most of us and less materialistic and very devout. President Carter's sister Ruth Carter Stapleton is a faith healer. A lady of the Church obtaining healing powers through prayers, and of course the most astounding and blessed healer around — with a very large sphere of activity — is our Mother Theresa inspired by a direct perception of Christ, and an inspiration to millions. The art or science of Spirit Healing expects to gain popularity in the near future in this country as men grow more and more sensitive and develop allergies and psychosomatic troubles which, present drugs can relieve but rarely cure permanently. For, after all, Spirit Healing is ancient knowledge — a jnan' received by the sensitive primitive men living in the bosom of Nature and capable of revelatory experience. Today 'Vigyan' tends towards materialism in the eyes of the common man, who tends to reject his own soul and spirit with his conscious mind. But this 'Vigyan' is also developing psychiatry, psychology and para-psychology —and the enlightened among the educated know that the subconscious mind has capabilities that Yogis and great men use, and that more and more people will use, as humanity evolves. These capabilities include creativity, which overindulgence in materialism often suppresses and the ability to have psychic experiences even without the help of hypnosis or drugs. Yoga is so popular today for it helps man develop his inner power and takes away his more violent urges which today's materialistic lifestyle fosters.

"Most spirit healers are highly infinitive and psychic—they are often clairvoyant to a high degree, although they do not trust their own clairvoyance when it comes to voicing themselves openly. Often their spirit friends or Guides discourage predictions."

Are you not surprised that a patient of mine should take so much interest in healing and write for different publications? This she has obviously done after referring several patients to me for absent healing.

Mrs. Indrani is not the only journalist who has helped me in my cause. I had the unique pleasure of meeting an equally versatile personality: Miss Janet Fine who is in India for some months now doing research on psychic phenomena in our country. She has travelled throughout India and has written for many publications. She was introduced to me by a doctor and she was highly impressed with my healing work. She is not only an accomplished classical dancer of Bharatanatyam and Kathak but also an author of two books—one on Aura and the other on healing. Miss Janet Fine is the proud daughter of Dr. Benjamin Fine who was very close to Einstein. She is herself a powerful medium with a rare gift of healing and vibrations. She has not only received healing vibrations from me but has also given me healing for my aching joints. In spite of being an American, Janet can speak and write Hindi and knows much more about our country, our religion and culture than an Indian can expect a 'foreigner' to know.

According to Paul Solomon, man does not usually either recognise or believe that he is endowed with capabilities far beyond those accepted as being normal. Solomon feels that it is his mission in life to help people to transcend these limitations and realise their true potential as spiritual beings. Most sages and teachers speak of an inner light or voice that guides us on our journey through life. In order to follow this light, we must first become aware of its existence and aware of the temptations and delusions that trap the unwary on their way. It is a pity that millions of rupees go down the drain every year for research done in pharmaceutical products. Let it be known that not a single rupee is allotted to the research in healing of a different kind—a method which is far superior, safer and of course beneficial.

The cardinal rule of health professed by the healer is: "Keep a quiet, contented mind. Train yourself in the habit of meeting emergency with calmness, never giving way to brooding and worry. Avoid, as poisonous and suicidal, anger and fear."

A very interesting book dealing with Psychic Healing, entitled *Healing Hands*, was written by J. Bernard Hutton, a hardened journalist who, stricken by threatened blindness, came across the medium, George Chapman, and his Spirit control, the late Dr. William Lang, through whom his sight was fully restored. Hutton was so stunned that he studied all available evidence about Chapman's work and discovered that there were thousands of cases like his, which were treated with unfailing results. Hutton said in his book that there was much more to present an unbiased and authentic account of Chapman's work. He therefore travelled several thousand miles in Britain to interview the patients he had picked out at random from Chapman's files of case histories. He also tape-recorded statements from people who were cured. Some claimed that they had been cured completely from diseases which hospital doctors had said were incurable. "Apart from interviewing patients, I also checked their statements and medical histories. I wanted to be fully satisfied that I was in possession of facts and not highly coloured (and possibly inaccurate) accounts."

Says Hutton and further asserts:

> Every patient's name and place of residence published in the book is authentic.

Dr. Edwards Townley Bailey, in his introduction to the book, called it a "True story of miracles wrought by spirit healing through the devoted partnership of two men—a famous consultant-Surgeon: William Lang — who lived in the 19th and early 20th century". Dr. William Lang is known to a number of doctors living even today — as also to his medium George Chapman. Both these men were able to apply healing powers which are not within the range of ordinary treatment.

"Most doctors know only too well the limitation of their ability to relieve sickness and suffering and this book should indeed help them to see the genuineness of spirit healing and it's potentialities. All that has been related here is a presentation of proven facts. I am convinced that the miracles described are not figments of the imagination. I know how hard it is for doctors to accept that which is not verifiable by the usual methods of assessment, but this book is one that should stimulate both doctors and patients to further unbiased inquiry. The greater the initial scepticism, the deeper will be the final conviction. I have no hesitation in saying that, from my own experience in my surgical career, I accept without question that miracles can and do happen under conditions so faithfully presented by Hutton."

Dr. Bailey is unquestionably an eminently great surgeon who has made a distinctive mark in the medical profession by his surgery.

> With regard to the miracle question, I can only say that the word 'impossible' is not, to my mind, applicable to matters of philosophy. That the possibilities of nature are infinite is an aphorism with which I am wont to worry my friends.
>
> —*Professor huxley*

> A presumptuous scepticism that rejects facts without examination of their truth, is, in some respects, more injurious than unquestioning credulity. —*Humboldt*

18

Harry Edwards, the World's Most Famous Healer: A Tribute

As he had foreseen and expected, Harry Edwards passed away in the early hours of December 9,1976. Although all his colleagues and friends had heard about his passing from him much in advance, they did not expect him to be as accurate about the time and the day of the last journey, as he was always accurate in diagnosing the diseases at the mere touch of his fingertips on his patients' bodies. He was famous in "intuitive diagnosis" when difficult cases were referred to him. In each case his diagnosis was proved right. This convinced the doctors that one can be "in tune" with whatever that "something" is: the something that to Harry Edwards, was spiritual healing.

After all, such fields as physiotherapy and hypnosis as well as psychiatry, were for any years frowned on as unwanted intruders. Today they are widely accepted and so will be spiritual healing.

His physical loss in sleep brought tears to the eyes of thousands of his patients as they saw their 'spirit doctor' with an irresistible smile on his lips, in an eternal sleep. His message to me shall remain an unforgettable tribute from a rare friend I had on the physical plane:

> My dear Doctor Keni.... I have completed my duty on this plane, I am so glad you are doing the healing work so efficiently and sincerely. You will now have one more

> Guide to help you —me...Harry Edwards. You are now rightly my co-worker. My blessings to you, my child.

Born in London on May 29, 1893, he was the eldest of nine children. After completing his schooling at the Noel Park Council School, Wood Green he entered into an apprenticeship as a compositor. Three years later he became the Hon. Secretary to the North Lambeth League of Young Liberals and continued active service in politics until 1935. He moved to India in 1915 and saw active service on the N. W. Frontier. In 1917 he moved into N. W. Persia reaching the rank of a Major, commanding the Garrison Troops and so also a Director of Labour. In 1929 he contested the Parliamentary Election for the North-West Camberwell and commenced his healing ministry as a spare-time occupation. In 1944 he moved to Burrows Lea and devoted his whole time to healing. In 1955 he received his first millionth letter on absent healing and also did his first Television Programme. Maurice Barbanell, the author of several books on Spiritualism and Editor of *Psychic News* and *Two Worlds* rightly said about Harry Edwards:

> The first 25 years of his life, when he sought for a political career had been a failure. How happy we are that instead of being an M.P. he became the Prime Minister of Healing.

Edwards, who included members of Britain's Royal Family among his thousands of patients, had received incontrovertible evidence of at least two of his spirit cooperators: Pasteur and Lister, who both made outstanding contributions to medicine in their days.

His healing success had brought him deserving world fame. No sooner he discovered that he was the chosen one with a Divine gift of healing, than he utilised it fully. There are few amongst us who have spent as large a part of the allotted span in such beneficent service to humanity. Unconsciously he came to such a fame as is given to few and yet it left no mark on him till the day he passed away.

He demonstrated his healing success in the largest halls in Britain which include the Royal Albert Hall and the Royal Festival Hall. Hundreds of thousands of people have witnessed his healing demonstrations in practically every part of Europe.

At the Harry Edwards Spiritual Healing Sanctuary of Burrows Lea, at Surrey in England, countless patients suffering from 'incurable' diseases have been treated to the amazement of world-famous medical men. Rightly he never took credit for himself of the tremendous number of cures, realising that he was the instrument of higher spirit powers whose beneficent purpose is to heal the sick. Most of these were after they were told that medically "there is no hope for them". An increasing number of doctors sought his aid for themselves and their patients — secretly though!

This white-haired handsome man who has done more than anyone to put healing on the map from his famous Sanctuary, deep in the snow-clad Surrey Countryside, had to be seen to be believed for his dedication and simplicity which made him the world's greatest healer who chose to spend his life in a world of sickness and sorrow.

In addition to a fine collection of ivory, rare books and a fine zest for living, he had also a sense of humour. On was struck with his absolute sincerity and freedom from any kind of egotism or self-consciousness. A man of character with child-like faith and a deep wisdom, an astringent quality in his challenges yet gentle and kindly, his physical presence will be greatly missed. His passing has created a void in our lives which no one else can fill. What a happy time the spirit world must have enjoyed preparing that very gallant gentleman for the glorious work of healing and how their heart must have rejoiced as they saw him giving each year hop and health to thousands of sad and weary ones struggling under their load of suffering!

The five oak saplings planted by him flanking the southern border of Burrows Lea in 1953 have grown into sturdy trees There was a happy affinity between the growth of these sturdy trees and the flourishing development of healing so sturdy trees and the flourishing development of healing so much of which has stemmed from Burrows Lea and the man with whom this place will always be associated.

SECTION TWO

19

Introduction

Dear reader: I feel extremely happy to be with you today, for I can tell you why and how to live a better mental, psychic, emotional and physical life.

I do not boast of giving you an all-perfect life, though my research and experience during the past 40 years or so of quest in the fields of parapsychology, psychic healing, and ESP, have brought to me stark realities that I would like to share with you.

I firmly believe that the human being is essentially meant to live at peace with himself and the world, with a deep sense of joy and harmony. I would ardently wish and pray that the heart of every person should experience a total celebration of life, light, joy, peace, harmony and love, rather than a long funeral. There is surely not a problem-free Camelot or a painless Utopia and yet, the glory of God is present in the one, who is fully "alive" at all places, all the time.

We are sad because very few of us are aware of our full potential and our waiting "possibilities." The average person accomplishes less than, let it be said, only 10 per cent of his/her promise. We see hardly 5 per cent of the beauty in the world around us. We have perhaps heard only about 5 per cent of the beautiful music and poetry in the world. We have smelt but a fraction of the world's irresistible fragrance. Our hearts are only 10 per cent alive with joy and love; we are only 5 per cent open to our emotions. We die, quite unfortunately, without ever having lived or really loved many or much.

Each one of you is a double mystery—the mystery of yourself and the mystery of the body you are in. The body is the lock and you are the key to the lock. The purpose of this is to remind you how to understand yourself as the key to the mystery to your self and how to locate yourself in your body, how to find and know your real Self *as* Self-knowledge, how to use yourself as the key to open the lock to the body and, through your body, how to understand and know the mysteries of nature and natural things.

When you solve this mystery as a doer of your self-knowledge, and the operator of your body-machine, you will know in each detail—and altogether—the function of the units of your body and the laws of nature enclosing it and functioning through it. Consequently, you will be able to work in harmony with the great Nature-Machine through its individual body-machine in which you are.

Let me deal now with the mind, which has no centre of location within the body. It appears to be everywhere—in the muscles, tissues, cells, bones, and in the various organs. There is no separation between the mind and consciousness: both operate psychically. When you encounter something that is too negative or confusing to deal with, the knowledge that you have chosen it for your own learning experience will make it less difficult for you to cope with.

The task then becomes an attempt at an investigation into the *why*'s of events, so that the pieces can be easily treated against the larger picture. The most important thing in life is: you should have absolutely no regrets for anything you might have done in the past, no regrets whatsoever. Remember that our thoughts influence the course and outcome of an illness. We therefore have to re-train the mind to avoid negative thought-traps and thus open ourselves up to nature, to spiritual forces, and to divinity.

You would perhaps like me to tell you something about the health and power of the mind. Health can be defined as "inner peace", letting go of fear of any kind and in any form, of all negative thoughts, and replacing these with unconditional love for all things and persons. Love, in the truest sense of the word, is absolutely unconditional, expecting nothing in return for all the giving: that is the way God loves us and that is the way we must love others. There are *no* doubts in this form of love, but only after a total acceptance of the "other." The fear of death, of the future, of pain, of losing someone very dear to us (all of which are in the subconscious), are, unfortunately, at the top of our list of priorities. Every one of us should learn to accept anything that comes along, even without our least conscious effort. Generally, we lose control over our perception of things. If we are to find total peace of mind in the midst of contemporary chaos, we need to love instead of fear, to realise that we do not *have* to be sick, lonely or deprived. We can learn to be fully responsible for anything we see and experience.

It is possible to change even a deeply ingrained belief-structure, by shifting your focus away from the fear of all the past preconceptions or future "unknowns." One reason why this is so is that worry, feelings of guilt, fear, doubt, lack of faith and all those negative emotions drain us of the energy that could have been preserved and used to nourish our mind and body. Negativity is totally incapacitating. If you spend your whole life determining what is impossible or difficult, it limits your knowledge as to what is possible. And that makes it tough enough to tap our normal energies. We all have to believe—and really believe, with our soul—that it is possible for us to achieve a perfect, undisturbed peace of mind. And we have got to want it so badly that we can almost taste it. Unfortunately, most of us come to this conviction only through trying times.

Please remember that there is a way to look at the world through a spiritual lens. You must refuse to think yourself as a "victim", blaming the whole world for *your* unhappiness. You must begin to change from an angry, uncompromising or sad person to a vibrant individual who must begin to locate joy and pleasure, peace and happiness in the most unlikely way—through helping others. You should, immediately *and* ultimately, find the key and the link between the mind and the body.

Do it seriously, with an open mind. You will realise that finally LOVE has alone all the might and power in this universe. Once you tap on to it, you become one with the "Universal, Cosmic, Energy-Force": with this power, nothing is impossible. What we need is an occasional miracle to happen in our lives to help us realise that anything is possible. If we look forward to such miracles with an open mind, we shall find them.

The other important thing in order to achieve better physical, mental, emotional and spiritual life, is *to learn to forgive*. Forgiveness is the key to individual happiness and peace of mind. Unfortunately, most of us miss our chances to forgive. And it is not enough to forgive someone for having done something you disagreed with. You have to go much deeper and further than that. You must *forgive yourself* for your misconceptions about the other person, for judging that person and not seeing him or her as a human being.

The thought should be that there is no disease, no pain, no disorder, but only health, well-being, peace and comfort, where diseases lie in a subtle, breath-form. Mental efforts and a deep faith would be the right way in curing your "disease", making it possible for you to will that "disease" away.

You have heard me laying emphasis on love. Indeed the whole human family should be bathed in an element of love, like delicately fine ether enveloping and seeping though everything. Good friendships and sincere, pure relationships are a result of *unconditional* love; it is what blood is to the body. When the link of a friendship or relationship is disturbed, love dies too, and out of this death, hatred and resentment are born. Let therefore a normal dialogue return. Let the hearts—rather than the minds—speak. This will offer a new life to a dead relationship. There are no winners or losers in this dialogue of love: there are always winners. Dialogue is essentially an act of the unconditional and pure love. This alone is the real secret of staying in love, peace, light and harmony.

You should never ever feel alone. Your "thinker" and your "knower" are always with you. On the ocean or in a forest, on mountains or plains, in sunlight or shadow, in a crowd or in solitude—wherever you may be—your thinking-and-knowing self is with you. Your real Self will protect you in so far as you will allow yourself to be protected. Whatever you have made for yourself as your "destiny", you must learn the two great lessons which all the experiences of life finally come together to teach us: what to do and what not to do.

Lastly, let me tell you about the purpose behind every disease and ailment. The purpose is to purge the body and the breath-form and to force the sufferer to learn. A portion of certain thoughts is focussed as a disease in order to purge the body and thereby, through the four systems in the body, to purge the breath-form. The purging of the body is accompanied by a process of boiling out when time and condition form a juncture. The "boiling out" is what is called a disease. The sores and ulcers and festerings are the visible scum brought out by the seething. The other purpose of disease is to force the sufferer to learn a particular thing. Ailments are therefore usually accompanied by pain, fear, weariness, despondency, disabilities of various kinds including discomforts and inconveniences. All these affect the feeling of the doer directly through the nerves of the body.

Disease teaches the doer what not to think and what not to do. Its purpose is not to teach the doer what it should think and what it should do. We all live in a vast ocean of Cosmic Force. We know it and we can understand it we care to study the life of a tree. Whether it is a tree or any vegetation, it lives not merely from the nourishment of the soil. They all receive *prana* or poser of good or cosmic force of which the rays of the sun are just one example. Humans, plants, trees and animals receive cosmic forces sub-consciously all the time to remain healthy.

I give maximum importance to *pranayama* which was practised by all the holy men and which is mentioned in almost all the scriptures and so also our ancient medical systems. *Pranayama*, therefore, is one of the methods of receiving the cosmic forces through breathing. Its entry is situated in the nasal cavity, from where a ductless glandular system proceeds to the brain, the pineal gland, the endocrine gland and a number of other very important and vital glands, while its main trunk follows alongside the spinal column. From here it divides off and permeates every part of our body. We should, consciously and with intention, be manipulators of energy that passes through us all the time.

One of the most useful discoveries in psychology was made by Dr. F. W. H. Myers around in 1886. The discovery asserted the fact that the subconsciousness contains a dust heap and so also a treasure house, that is, two opposite forces. The Dust Heap contains all kinds of suppression and repression. These are obviously of harmful kind and they choose to remain together as true, loyal friends. They include conditions like manias, fits, malice, evil thoughts, negative and unhealthy emotions, dangerous impulses including nervous breakdowns. If left alone, they succeed in conquering the will. Fear, for instance, is factually a potential destroyer of our happiness. In the other force, namely, the Treasure House, there are ambitions, positive thoughts, good urges and talents, higher aspects of life, artistic impulses and of course rich experiences of spiritual guides and saints.

These all combine and work together and when a chance is given, they will pervade the consciousness with a feeling of good health, joy, courage and confidence. For its own protection the mature mind remains a careful optimist about humanity, studying the evolving pattern of man's progress. It notices that good invariably triumphs over evil. It constantly practises positive thinking knowing that imagination acts up on the mind more powerfully than any other forces. It develops this quality and it tries to keep the imagination charged with a feeling broad optimism. It realises and fully knows that negative thoughts are not only useless but dangerous and that they consume mental energy in abundance and produce only depressing and gloomy-mind-patterns.

The range and interests of the mature mind are wide and they are carefully and purposefully cultivated. Nothing is ugly or useless for a mature mind. When personally attacked by sorrow, suffering or injustice, those with a mature mind remain courageous without the slightest bitterness. Behind every aspect of life, they seek a pattern and purpose and they are able to illustrate their implicit faith with evidence when they are faced with the doubt of the agnostic. They have a careful integrity, holding fast to ideals and standards, endeavouring to be true in love, and always loyal in friendship.

Guild is yet another cause of neurotic and mental disease. Those with mature minds successfully escape self-guilt ; but if they fail, they do learn to forgive themselves when they fall short of their own ideals. They refuse to run away from life because they accept life with all its problems and compensations. They are conscious of the constancy and immutability of natural laws and divine wisdom that the universe (including all of us of course) is subject to inflexible ordinances. Cause and effect, or sowing and reaping are the means by which everything is thoroughly and methodically controlled with justice and wisdom. They know that just as the seasons automatically follow one another, so does human conduct produce its inevitable result. They do not take the operation of natural law for granted but realise what chaos would result if only the four seasons got out of their cycle or if the earth ceased to revolve even for a few moments. The well-being of the human mind, its power to act to bear hardships and to progress cheerfully, depends on man's ability to reduce as much as possible, the Dust Heap in his consciousness and to charge his being, with more and more life-giving energy, by remaining in harmony, with nature, maintaining an internal calm that including mind, body and soul, thus storing up in himself the abundant treasure one's mind is capable of absorbing.

20

ESP and Life after Death

We should be thankful to the labours and the most heroic fortitude of a large number of people who have stood for the establishment of the fact life does exist beyond the grave in the face of hostility and even some times persecution. It is of course not a new revelation so much as a reemergence of something as old as humanity itself. One of the exponents of the cause was the great Lord Brougham who, in the fifties of the nineteenth century, uttered an oft-quoted remark regarding modern spiritualism and its purpose. He rightly compared it to the rising of semi-could in the skies of scepticism. The most convincing facts have come from men and women held very high in the world's esteem and who have boldly pursued the inquiry and dared to proclaim their faith.

John Scott is the most familiar name in the spiritual world who has also been one of the outstanding writers. He was highly sceptical of his psychic faculty until it first manifested. He received many striking communications in automatic writing and then came the overwhelming evidence, confirmed by mediums who did not know him, that the communicator was none other than Lord Curzon-famous as statesman and administrator.

Well known are the trance-utterances of J.J. Morse who is one of the greatest of trance mediums. Proofs of manifestation and messages from the world of the beyond are no more controversial. The proofs have been convincingly persistent we have the examples of Sir Oliver Lodge, Sir William Barrett. W. T. Stead (the most brilliant journalist of his age), G.R.S. Mead, Rec. Arthur Chambers and a host of others.

Tennyson, who was a great poet, who knew a good deal about spiritualism, put the matter in inimitable way in his lines in the Ring. It surely makes fitting epilogue:

> Even so the Ghost in Man, the Ghost that once was Man, are calling to each other thro' a dawn stranger than earth has ever seen : the veil is rending and the voices of the dead are heard across the voices of the dark. No sudden heaven, nor sudden hell for man. But thro' the Will of One who knows and rules and utter knowledge is but utter love— Aeonian Evolution, swift or slow. Thro' all the spheres—an ever opening height, an ever lessening earth.

Communication between the two worlds- between the living and the dead, as they are rather inaccurately called, for the dead are the more living of the two-which has gone on through all the ages in a more or less sporadic fashion is, in these modern times, has begun on a new phase more —continuous, more convincing, more orderly and of course more organised than ever before.

There have been hundreds of books in evidence suggesting convincingly life after death. These books with the Authors' sincere and elaborate research have revealed new phenomena and given us more and more details and insight into what has been called "the great unknown":

Death-bed Visions by W.F Barrett, *Life After Death* by C.S. A. Ducasse, *The Enigma of Survival* by H. Hart, *Life Without Death* by N. Jacobson, *Life After Life* by R.A. Moody, *Not Silent if Dead* and *The Dead-active* by Mrs. A.L. Fernie, From the Other Side by S.H.D. Miller, *Thirty Years Among the Dead* by C.A. Wickland, *The Great Reality* by J. H. Remmers, *Survival: a Fact?* by Margaret Hamilton, *Re-incarnation: Based on Facts* by Karl Muller and one of the latest and best books which I have read on the subject is *At the hour of Death* by Karls Osis and Erlenour Haraldson, with a bold introduction by Elisabeth Kubler-Ross. M.D., who has rightly said that it is a book that all researchers and scientists should read if they have questions and problems with the widely publicised research on death and life after death.

There is no doubt that there is survival after death. A physically enveloped body is something more than a physiological complex with an intricate nervous system. It is the *Atma*—an inner presence, immanent and animating, transcendent and imperishable. Life is not a transitory futility. Death is not total annihilation. It is a door to the discarnate persistence of personhood. Astral projection, during and departing from bodily chapter, is an index of the non-carnate entity in us. Liberation from illusion, understanding the relativity of things around and the attainment of Supreme knowledge gained in glimpses of higher consciousness—such is the next goal of man as a pilgrim of progress in a super-Darwinian leap of evolution aided by a bolder intuition of science.

"Graveyards are merely receptacles for discarded suits, the reverence paid to them is truly pathetic"

The best-known cartoonist of *Daily Mirror,* who has spent practically the whole of his adult life studying world religions and philosophies, writes:

> You know as surely as I do that we never die. We merely change Nothing ever dies in this world. It just changes back into the atoms of which it was originally composed. We are all connected with this Supreme Mind through the subconscious — that mind or part of mind that never sleeps.
>
> That part of mind is in touch with the Great Essence. That part of mind, through the Great Essence keeps the body alive. It is the mind that dies. It is the body that dies. The spirit is indestructible. We have all come from the spirit world and we all have to return to it. When the span of life is over and we are ready to die, all our pain and discomfort disappear. We find ourselves drifting away from our earthly bodies—drifting upward like a captive balloon, floating there for a while looking down on the now empty body, stretched out on the bed.

Canon P.D. Pearce-Higgins, Vice-Provost of South Wark, makes no secret of his psychic convictions that are based on his personal experiences of mediumship. Not long ago he accepted a novel challenge to lecture to the agnostic members of the National Secular Society on "The Evidence of Survival After Death". In his address he has detailed the philosophical reasons why an "after-life" is logical. Then he showed that he had added knowledge to his faith through proofs that scientists had obtained through mediumship.

No one was more surprised than Bligh Bond, when his distant relative, Captain William Bligh of Mutiny of the Bounty fame, returned and bridged the gap of more that two centuries. Bligh, concerned to rehabilitate himself, was accompanied by members of his crew, who were equally determined to end the many travesties which described him as a sadistic tyrant. They all communicated in automatic writing through Mrs. Jessie Stevens- an American Medium at Seances that began in 1933. Bligh's communications were even more dramatic than the mutiny of April 22, 1789 and his subsequent epic journey of 3,000 miles with 17 companions in an open boat.

They were beast with perils and menaced by lack of food and water before they reached Tahiti. Bligh Bond, with his long experience of mediumship, considered the Spirit-return of his relative to be possibly the most startling and significant of his psychic experiences. Seance experiments, unlike those performed in our chemical laboratories, are not constant. Emotional energy of the psychic variety cannot be stored in a pipette, nor can it be measured in grams/ounces. Nevertheless, any researcher, sympathetically primed by psychic knowledge is bound to receive maximum cooperation from the guides or other available controls of a medium. Elaborate systems of theology, primarily based on the spirit-return of some well-loved persons were built hundreds of years ago to supplement this basic human craving for personal continuity after death.

According to Maurice Barbanell, who has spent more than forty years of his life making research on psychic phenomena and who is considered an authority on the subject, has been able to collect sufficient material for a book on the psychic life of Edger Wallace:

> My search produced a fascinating sequel. Wallace as you will see, was a born psychic, who also wrote after his passing a remarkable script describing spirit life as he found it. He became the central character in a true-to-life-and-death story which was even more dramatic than the ingenious plots of his thrillers.

With the cooperation of Geraldine Cummins, the world's greatest automatic writing medium, a series of articles were communicated through his hand.

If the life of the individuals is merely an interlude between nothingness before conception and nothingness after death, if we are only sparks of consciousness who shine for an instant in the infinite and eternal darkness, then we shall naturally try to live as long as possible even to the extent of prolonging the painful process of dying. But if we know that life persists after death we shall not be haunted by the fear of annihilation or obsessed by the need to ward off death at all costs. On the contrary, we shall welcome death as we welcome sleep at the end of the day!

21

The Healer as a Vehicle

A basic principle of the universe is that nothing moves or happens without the use or application of some form of energy. A vehicle needs to be physically pulled or propelled by fuel. The wind blows and stirs the leaves. Electrical energy gives light and power. Even in the action of a chemical or an emotion a form of energy is released. It must therefore follow, that the work of the Spirit needs some "form of energy" to make an activity possible. Ray Branch, a healer, writes:

> Ask a physicist to write down a formula of Spirit energy and he could not, because it is something outside the realms of earthly scientific terms as we understand them. However, the results can indeed by evaluated, insofar as they can be demonstrated, as we so often see when an arthritic joint that has been fixed for years is able to move again: or a growth clearly shown on an earlier X-ray is now no longer present. Again, we see such results when, for instance, vision is restored following the dispersal of a cataract or in restoration of hearing to a deaf ear or when the young agoraphobic is able to go and enjoy a crowded Saturday-night disco. Obviously a major change for the better has been brought about.

The energies from Spirit are just as capable of undergoing conversion as are our accepted scientific energies. But can these Spirit energies, from a totally different dimension, also undergo conversion?

Let us consider what happens when we are dealing with the healing of a physical illness such as arthritis. A joint become locked. It has become calcified. There is a build-up of calcium carbonate that prevents movement, causing great pain. Obviously the joint cannot be moved until the obstructing material has been taken away. In a great majority of cases, a change for the better comes about through us. I say 'through us' because we do not do the healing, and further more, we do not know precisely how to do it. So what is the part we play in the healing endeavour? The answer is that we are able to open ourselves as transformers of those Spirit energies I have mentioned, and we do this through our capacity for attainment with the healers in Spirit. I am not going into the why's and wherefore's of attunement, because it is a complex subject on its own. So let us just say that you, as the healer in this case, have allowed your psychical mind to recede so that your spirit mind become ascendant and therefore open to impressions and directions from your spirit helpers. Above all, you are open, as it were, to that free flowing of the Spirit-directed energies that are needed to accomplish this particular healing task.

Let us assume that in a very short while the joint has become freed and the patient's pain overcome through the intervention of spirit-directed energies on a physical condition composed, in this case, of the chemical, calcium carbonate, which has now been dispersed. In a few seconds it has undergone a major chemical change, which was not possible through medical science.

In order for that Spirit energy to act upon the physical illness, it has to be converted into a physical energy. This is where the healer plays a vital part in being used as a sort of 'chemical laboratory', acting as a transformer of energy, although we do not know the precise process whereby the spirit energy is converted into a physical energy.

Let us consider the implication of the healing that has taken place:

1. The patient has felt no pain and from this itself we conclude that some form of spirit energy has had the effect of a local anaesthetic at the initial stage.

2. The joint that may have been fixed for months or years is freed in a matter of seconds, which leads us to a number of conclusions:
   a) There has been a diagnosis of some intense depth, analysing the precise structure of the harmful chemical deposit that has been corroding and fixing the joint.
   b) The diagnosis has been made in a matter of seconds without any prior knowledge of the patient's medical history, without X-rays or any record of drug intake and so on.
   c) Following the diagnosis, there has come about almost in an instant of time, a building up of counter energies that have been amalgamated and applied in a precisely ordered way upon the diseased area, leaving all other adjacent tissues untouched. When we think of the complexity of the healing process at work in this one hypothetical case, it shows beyond any doubt, that healing is a very advanced Spirit science, the operative speed of which belittles our most sophisticated computer.

Just as we know that there are various forms of energy in our earthly science, so it follows that there are various forms of energy in Spirit science as well. There are the dispersing energies I have written about, and these themselves can be broken down into varying characteristics, because there is no doubt that the energies required to disperse growth must be different in nature for those needed to clear, let us say, a cataract or those that are employed to build up essential nutrients in the blood for example, in cases of leukaemia. There are the other vital energies that act directly upon what we call the bodily intelligence systems to activate the endocrine systems for a whole range of glandular and digestive diseases. These energies themselves can by subdivided into those needed to ant upon the central nervous system in cases of stroke and paralysis with further subdivision of energies acting directly upon the Spirit mind of the patient where there may be a need to bring about a change in outlook from, say one of sadism to kindliness.

According to Harry Edwards who is considered one of the world's greatest spiritual healers, the secret of healership and that of holy men, was that they did learn the way in which they could consciously take in their fill of the *Pranic* forces to sustain their physical needs and faculty of taking in these unseen forces. This involves the use of a bodily mechanism, closely associated with our ductless glands. Medical science knows these but does not know enough about them, their purpose or how they work.

Pranayama is one of the methods of receiving the cosmic forces through breathing. Its entry is situated in the nasal cavity from where a ductless glandular system proceeds to the brain, the pineal gland, the endocrine gland and a number of other vital glands, while its main trunk runs along the spinal column. From here it divides off and permeates every part of our body. Harry Edward writes:

> How can we induce a good take-in of these forces? The way of doing this is not easy to describe in words, but we can see the way by illustration. When one goes to the seaside, one becomes aware of some unusual quantities in the ozone. So we inhale it fully, having that inner sense or knowledge that it is good for us. We fill up our lungs consciously and purposefully, taking in the goodness and strength of cosmic forces contained within the air, from the sea. While the sea air contains special cosmic properties, these beneficial forces are in the atmosphere everywhere, even in an industrial town. We take them in subconsciously every time we breathe—just as do the trees. But to absorb additional supplies of '*Prana*', to fill to overflowing our reservoirs of energy, we must seek this purposefully. So just as we fill ourselves with ozone-laden air at the seaside, so we could consciously and with intention invite in the cosmic forces. It is an exercise linked with our intelligence. Most of the healers who quite naturally take in an abundance of *Prana* are usually radiant in health and when they visit a sick one, the patient does feel better for the visit. What actually happens is that for their sympathy for the sick, consciously or subconsciously, a flow of power is directed in abundance to the patient. Most of the healers learn to do this in order to give to their inner strength and to refill themselves later. If they do not, then they too, can feel depleted.

Kirlian photography portrays a vivid picture which is indicative of such passing of energy from a healer to the patient but it is only a picture of the flow of energy. In fact, this flow of energy is very much present in a perennial motion, that is manipulated in a particular fashion through and influencing field which a healer creates. The creation of such an influencing field inevitably prevails without which it would not be possible for a healer to effect any cure. Elaborate research in the past few years of an electromagnetic shield around all living organisms and the influence of the energy fields also support the above views.

Awarded a Nobel Prize for this work on medical, parapsychological and scientific research, Dr. Alexis Carrel writes of the effect of the spirit on the human body:

— Certain spiritual activities may cause anatomical as well as functional modifications of the tissues and organs. These organic phenomena are observed in various circumstances, among them being the state of prayer. Prayer should be understood not as a mere mechanical recitation of formulas, but as a mystical elevation, an absorption of consciousness in the contemplation of a principle both permeating and transcending our world.

— The prayer which is followed by organic effects is of a special nature. Generally, the patient who is cured not praying for himself, but for another and prayer may set in motion a strange phenomenon the miracle.

— Our present conception of the influence of prayer upon pathological lesions is based upon the observation of patients who have been cured almost instantaneously of various afflictions such as tuberculosis, colds, abscesses, suppurating wounds, lupus and so on. The process of healing changes little from one individual to another. Often, an acute pain, then a sensation of being cured. In a few seconds, a few minutes, at the most a few hours, wounds are cicatrised, pathological symptoms disappear, appetite returns. Sometimes symptoms disappear, appetite returns. Sometimes symptoms vanish before the anatomical lesions are repaired.

— The miracle is chiefly charcterised by an extreme acceleration of the process of organic repair. There is no doubt that the rate of cicatrisation of the anatomical defects is much greater than the normal one. The only condition indispensable to the occurrence of the phenomenon is prayer. There is no need for the patient himself to pray, or even to have any religious faith. It is sufficient that someone around him be in a state of prayer.

Such facts are of profound significance. They show the reality of certain relations of still unknown connection between psychological and organic processes. They prove the objective importance of spiritual activities which hygienists, physicians, educators and sociologists have almost always neglected to study. They open to man a new world!

Food for Thought

We are taught from childhood that there are many subtle forces and forms of energy in nature which may be used by man. To the illiterate, there is as much mystery and awe about electricity as about psychic forces. In effect, he sees them as varying forms of the same thing and respects them both.

A little reflection may prove its worth. All energy and force is a manifestation of *Prana,* which means the basic energy or "soul" Oriental teachings say *Prana* has a mind behind it and that it emerges from the mind principle of the universe.

I believe, if we followed nature's laws, there would be no need for healing of any sort for all would maintain almost perfect health. But people deviate from nature and healing of some sort becomes necessary.

22

The Power of Thought

It is essential for all of us to understand what thought is.

Thought is a vibration. It is a very personal thing. It is firmly bound to the law of returns. Every thought goes out on the ether as a vibration, but does not forever vanish into the air. It remains attached to us, and by the Law of Returns comes back to the thinker. However, by the Law of Reciprocal Action, it will not just come back as it went out. It picks up similar thoughts on its way and when it returns, it often does so with devastating results. You should, therefore, be very careful about your thoughts which should be necessarily good, positive and nature ones. Today, by the thoughts we think, we are building our tomorrow.

You are aware that we come across or live with people with negative thoughts — people involved in jealousy, envy, backbiting, cynicism, and peevishness. Very often we mix with such people or we go out with them, eat with them on social visits. Mingling with such elements becomes sometimes inevitable and their negative and pessimistic thoughts about their illness, their woes, their troubles, do influence those with positive thoughts, bring mental and physical ailments unless one is able to reject them with positive force and will power.

We must not allow such things to operate against us or weigh us down. We must oppose all evil elements in order that our progress towards a happier and more hopeful and powerful condition of mind is not retarded. Remember that every thought of yours is a part of yourself, and if it is sent out in goodwill to one and all, it does meet the like current of thought, and mingling with it, finally takes current of thought, and mingling with it, finally takes the form of a gigantic current. It is far more potent than any material bond of communication. It is truly a LIVING FORCE, generating a real bond of communication and union between you and other like-minded souls.

We have accepted the fact that emotions affect our lives and that the negative emotions, like worry for instance, can cause not only ulcers, but also cancers. A telegram of a dear one's tragic accident or death, can manifest in a blanched face instantly, and often lead to total physical or mental collapse. This is not an uncommon episode in our hospitals. In the case of a person tragically bereaved, the entire body metabolism is disturbed, and thus weight may be consequently lost through actual tissue degeneration.

A treat or a feeling of threat of some kind is the most frequent cause of emotional upset. We have seen many who feel threatened by the loss of something of a sentimental value or religious importance, or by the loss of someone dear, loss of health loss of money and position, job or demotion. Unless we are not sure of our ability to meet such losses, new situations do arise, which seem to threaten us, ultimately causing a serious emotional upset.

This is because emotion alerts our nervous system by mobilising energy and making it possible to meet the threat with all our courage and will power.

It is a fact that one cannot make a good speech or render a good song, unless one is emotionally restrained. To run your fastest in a race, you have to be keyed up for it. However, emotion only helps if it stimulates us to think in advance of how we could cope with the situation, and tackle a situation aggressively when confronted by it.

Most of us can stand more emotion than we are likely to be called on to endure, but each of us has a breaking point. The nervous mechanism by which emotion is registered seems only capable of tolerating a certain amount of stimulation, and when this amount is exceeded, the functioning of the emotional mechanism becomes disorganised, and consequently, the person becomes emotionally upset.

It is necessary from the point of view of mental health that every person should learn to react well to feelings of threat of all kinds, in order that the emotion that is aroused may help to avoid developing more emotion than one can stand. It is very important to train oneself to react objectively whenever threatened. Consequently, one must think of what there is to do about the situation and take due action. This will make it possible for a person to react aggressively, and take whatever action is called for. If on one hand, one reacts subjectively, upsetting fears will crowd into the mind, and result in increasingly more emotion, and in all probability, in withdrawal from the threatening situation. Physical symptoms are bound to come, and those will cause increased alarm and worry. Ultimately, a subjective reaction to a threat is bound to cause illness.

The daring person, the courageous person, is not the one who is never afraid, but one, who faces situations that threaten instead of withdrawing from the confrontations. Well-developed aggressive attitudes bring about a general attitude which could be called the "Whatever happens I will meet it" attitude, which contrasts with the "I hope nothing happens" attitude prevailing when the withdrawal reaction is dominant. The former attitude brings composure and frees us from worry and fear that something may happen. We are ready to face it, if and when it comes. However, when the latter attitude is much stronger, we feel insecure as the chance of something happening will persist all the time. This attitude causes anxiety, fatigue, fear and other symptoms resulting from the anxiety.

A considerable percentage of disease and illness is directly attributed not only to emotions and feeling oi threat, but also to the stress and strain of modern living. There is increasing evidence to show that cancer has a basis in sustained emotional imbalance. Meanwhile, as the tempo of civilisation increases, the sensitive human organism is subjected to stress and strain far more intense now than in any previous times.

There is no doubt that if we lived perfect lives-free from the emotional bouts-we should be far more happy, placid, and much less prone to disease. Let us therefore cultivate the "Whatever-happens I will face it" attitude by expressing it at every opportunity. Let us pause as frequently as possible to consider the positive influences which is profoundly affecting our lives.

Tension dissolves if we blend with nature, the trees the fields, the scents, and the sounds of natural beauty with its splendid colours and illuminating sunshine. Perhaps we could value them more wisely if we realised in all seriousness, how vital to our physical and mental wholeness they have always been. You are a part of the supreme power and positive force which pervades and rules the universe. Consequently, you have the faculty of bringing to you by constant positive thought, positive desire and positive mental demand, increasingly more qualities, belongings and beneficial effects of this supreme power. Every positive thought thereafter is building for you something good for the future.

Some years ago, long and carefully conducted experiments carried out by the psychology faculty of a university in Sweden regarding the deeper aspects of the human mind, proved beyond doubt that even casual thoughts in the mind of the experimenter, were positively reactive on the subject's mind sufficient for one to confirm the popular dictum: Thoughts are Things. This is an ancient saying and according to old literature; even the great Greek philosopher Aristotle knew about it. That was as far back as the fifth century B.C. Aristotle was instrumental in discovering many psychological truths which stand just as firm today as when he evolved them. The most important is that the main function of man is action, while thought is his principal faculty. This fact is expressed in the modern psychology: "All thoughts, tend to work out in action unless countered by another thought." It is clear that action may not be always noticeable, though it may be just physical or psychosomatic in a bodily sense.

Aristotle, who virtually pioneered this field of activity, used to take nothing for granted to his theory, thought has two aspects: potential thought and actual thought. A thought is potential when it is only in the mind, but it becomes actual when expressed in matter. This is, therefore, a principle that applies to each and every thought capable of being manifested in, or through matter. However, the most important and effective part of the thought is its mental aspect: The Thought is the Soul of the Thing.

Famous astronomers have maintained that material objects are ephemeral, but thought forms can live forever. I would like to quote Horace Leaf on this subject:

> Thoughts living on their own account can become terribly potent, however, for they remain independent of the mind that made them, and unless one is watchful, they will enslave the thinker. History is filled with examples of this. I knew an inventor whose life bade fair to be ruined by such a thought. He developed the notion of making a new kind of key, and pondered on it so much, that it finally obsessed him, and brought his business and domestic life to a halt. His relief came when the thought eventually passed from potentiality to actuality through a dream and his invention became a material fact.

He further says,

> This truth is one which all spiritual healers would do well to bear in mind. Probably all human minds are aspects of the creative mind, and every thought, in its own field, may turn from potentiality to actuality, somewhere, somehow, resulting in good health through Spiritual Healing.

We come across, very often indeed, a number of sick persons whose sickness whose sickness exists only in their imaginations. Have we not heard the oft-mentioned saying: "It is all in the mind"? In other words the non-material part of our make-up does affect our general health considerably.

Today, because of wrong living, artificial surroundings, faulty diet, misplaced affection, loneliness and boredom, otherwise healthy people complain of "sickness" which cannot be diagnosed clinically as a disease or any illness. This really means that their illness is only in the mind, and this condition represents 80% of current sickness. Modern research has made it possible for us to know the effect of environment upon human development. It is a fact, that a normal being placed in a favourable environment, will under normal conditions maintain the natural inherent propensities to health and growth.

I cannot help quoting Sir Walter Scott on the power of thought—a message which should be enshrined in your mind all your life: "Thought power, meaning the right use, control direction and poser of thought known as New Thought, or the Science of Thought, sometimes termed 'the manipulation of thought currents', is of great assistance to serene and efficient living. The idea is to eliminate, as far as possible, such things as evil, hatred, limitations, fear, selfishness, ill-health, weakness and to concentrate upon and affirm their opposites, such as good, love, confidence, safety, understanding, strength and success."

It is a difficult process, but such thoughts, if faithfully persisted in, sink gradually into the subjective mind, where in time, they are said to work automatically to bring about happier conditions. Seeing the mind cannot hold two ideas simultaneously, the instant an undesirable thought occupies the mind, drive it out by dwelling upon its opposite virtue. This will prove more effective than strenuously willing the unwelcome thought to depart, which only tends to make it cling more tenaciously. Surely, this attitude would enhance the efficacy of spiritual healing. Control leads to content. So much of our day is usually wasted in useless emotions, anger, annoyances, irritations, without achieving anything except unnecessary wear and tear, and resenting circumstances that we could alter if we tried. Seeing our brain is a machine, we should not allow it to race along racking it to bits. We should see that it functions smoothly and thinking the thoughts we wish, sanely, logically and wholly.

23

Mental Healing: A Case History

Mental Healers is a precious book written by the unforgettable genius, Stefan Zweig and translated by Eden and Sedar Paul. It was first published by Cassell & Co. Ltd. of London. Stefan Zweig who had dedicated this book to Albert Einstein, writes about the tree greatest mental healers: Franz Anton Mesmer, Mary Baker Eddy and Sigmund Freud. I do not think it is necessary to write anything more than what is done by a score of authoritative writers about these researchers, particularly about Mesmer, who was unfortunately born a century too soon! However, he flourished over more than two centuries. In earlier days the medical world would have followed all his experiments with all seriousness and avid interest.

The unbiased mind of the middle ages had a definite serious place for things that were still capable of astonishment, with enough and more faith in things that were still capable of astonishment, with enough and more faith in things that stirred them than in any outward semblance. They were at once ready, and with an open mind and believed and accepted the so-called incomprehensible experiments. The philosophers of that era would not have considered Mesmer's experiments or doctrines absurd. On the contrary, they would have accepted the idea of macrocosm responding to microcosm, of world-soul communicating with the individual soul, of planets affecting and influencing the human body. They would have even taken for granted Mesmer's contention that one person acts in some mysterious way upon another by the magic of a will, competent to set the "fluid of animal magnetism" in motion.

Many of Mesmer's theories are now coming into line with more recent discoveries. We dare not deny that our nerves and senses are in some way influenced by external forces. Our word, even our whisper, is transmitted in a fraction of a second across oceans and continents, and we are taught and thus we learn day by day afresh that our ether is full of vibrations and other subtle substances and influences.

Mesmer's idea that our personality is the wellspring of an energy which radiates far beyond the limits of our bodily nerves in mysterious waves modifying other wills than our own are no more doubtful. Medical science then could only perceive the clockwork machinery of homosapiens. It could only discern that something had gone wrong with the organs and with the body which set the machinery in motion because it did not recognise the constructive and individual posers proper to the mind. The medical men could do nothing for those who suffered from nervous afflictions or those who were epileptic or those who suffered from mental aliments, yet brushed off Mesmer's experiments and efforts to relieve them by his magnetic method, a self-professes. Mesmer, however, remained patient and firm. His faith was not shaken claim or his work affected.

He was responsible for discovering psychology, hypnosis, suggestion or auto- suggestion, and psychoanalysis, even spiritualism and telepathy and yet he was a neglected man. But we are today reaping what he sowed. He was sentenced for his theories, but today we are honoured in their application and success.

Born in 1733, Franz Anton Mesmer became a Doctor of Medicine twice over in 1766. After following the latest discoveries in the realms of geology, physics, chemistry, law, mathematics, the arts, music. Until the day of his death in 1815, he continued his search for the universal driving poser indefatigably. According to Mesmer, illness is a disturbance of the harmony which should be present in the human organism. It is a pernicious interruption of the rhythmic tide of ebb and flow. Each individual however is equipped with posers to promote his or her health. These powers create in him the will-to- health, the undying and primitive vital urge expel all the illnesses from the body. It is the office of the new magnetic treatment which is presently called suggestive treatment, to increase this will-to health. Mesmer maintained throughout his experiments and research, that a desire to regain health can work miracles in the way of cure.

Now I could quote an interesting case history from *Mental Healers* by Stefen Zweig, which is not only convincing because it is well documented but also defines Mesmer's work.

A young girl named Maria Theresa Paradies at the age of four, had suffered from a sudden "paralysis of the optic nerve" which had made her, to all seeming, incurably blind. Since, from her tenderest youth she had a special gift as a pianist, the Empress took her up, granted the parents a pension of two hundred gold ducats and in addition had the child educated at her own cost. When she was a little older, Fraulein Paradies gave many concerts, one of which was attended by Mozart. (A great number of her compositions may be seen in manuscript in the facsimile format the Vienna Library.)

The girl was brought to Mesmer. Before this she had passed through the hands of the eminent specialist Professor Barth, famous for his operations on cataract, and she had been a regular patient of the court physician, Dr. Stoerk. Nothing they could do had any effect. But certain symptoms (conclusive twitching of the eyes which, at such times, bulged out of their sockets and disorders of the liver and spleen which, when acute, brought on attacks closely resembling mental alienation) lead us to believe that Fraulein Paradies's blindness was not caused by atrophy of the optic nerve but by a psychical disturbance. Mesmer was not slow to perceive that she must have suffered from some shock to the nervous system, and consequently hers was a case which might advantageously respond to his method of treatment. In order to follow the experiment closely, Mesmer took her into his house along with two other female patients and gave her magnetic treatment entirely free of cost.

So far, all Mesmer's contemporaries agree in their account. However during later years Mesmer's report of the case differs fundamentally from those of his colleagues. He declares that the girl's eyesight was almost completely restored, the other doctors insist that the supposed improvement was nothing but a trick and a figment of imagination.

Today, while this word "imagination" plays a decisive part in academic judgments concerning Mesmer, it is impossible for us, to voice a trustworthy judgement on such contradictory pronouncements. The fact that Maria Theresa paradies never again in later years was able to see, speaks in favour of the doctor's verdict in support of Mesmer. On the other hand, apart from public testimony given at the time, we have a manuscript report composed by the father of the girl, which to my way of thinking, is too circumstantial to be regarded as other than authentic.

The existing documents are so poignant a description of the gradual rediscovery of the world of light from which for long years the sufferer had been excluded, it would need a greater imaginative writer and psychologist than either poor old Herr Paradies or the practical minded Mesmer to invent such subtle observations and artificial moods. Here is the substance of the report:

> After a short magnetic treatment at the hands of Dr. Mesmer, she began to distinguish the contours of certain objects placed before her. The eyes were so sensitive that she could not bear to look at these objects when the room had been darkened by closing the shutters and drawing the curtains. She wore a five-fold bandage, and yet if a light were moved in front of this, she would fall to the ground as if struck by a thunderbolt. The first human being she saw was Dr. Mesmer. She looked at him for some time attentively, following the movements he made in order to test

> her eyes. She was somewhat put out by these movements and said: is horrid. Can that be the figure of a man? A housedog she had become attached to was brought in at her request. Again, very attentively, she contemplated this new apparition. "The dog", she said, "pleases me better than the man. His looks are far more agreeable to me". She was especially far more agreeable to me". She was especially amused by people's noses, and could not restrain her laughter whenever she beheld one saying: "They seem to be threatening me, and as if they wanted to pluck my eyes out."

After a while she grew accustomed to faces and did not find them so amiss. Her greatest difficulties were to learn the names of colours and to distinguish distances, for in the matter of sight, she was as ignorant as a new-born babe. She never made a mistake in the contrasted shades of colours, but committed many blunders when it came to naming them, especially if she was not put on the right trail by first comparing it to a colour she had learned to know.

When confronted with black, she declared it to be the picture of her former blindness. This colour invariable provoked her to a somewhat melancholy mood, a mood she was prone to during the course of treatment, when she would suddenly burst into tears for no apparent cause. Once she had such a bad attack, that tearing the bandage from her eyes, she threw herself upon the sofa, wringing her hands, groaning, and sobbing in the utmost despair, so that even Madame Saccor or any other famous tragedienne, could not have given a better display of extreme anguish. This pitiful condition passed away in a few minutes, and she speedily recovered her customary goods spirits. But the bad fit overwhelmed her shortly after.

During the early days of her recovery, she was much vexed by the numerous visits of relations, friends and notables. Once, in her displeasure, she said to me: "Why am I less happy than I used to be? Every fresh thing I see causes me an unpleasant sensation. I was far more peaceful in my mind when I was sightless." I confronted her with the assurance that she would then feel happier, that once she had grown used to seeing the world around her, all would be well again. That's a good thing, she answered, for if every fresh object were to continue to put me into such a state, I would infinitely rather return to my former blindness.

Since the restoration of sight placed her in a peculiarly untutored relation to the world around her, she could express her opinion without prejudice, just as the fancy took her. Her judgements of character after the contemplation of a person's face were singularly apt. She marvelled greatly when first shown a reflection in a mirror, not being able to understand how a flat surface of glass, could capture an object and then present it so that the eyes could behold it anew. She was taken to a room where a huge mirror almost covered one of he walls, and she was never weary of looking at herself therein. She posed before it and was especially amused, when she approached it or withdrew from it, to see herself performing.

Next morning she was led to the marble basin which she always called a big soup-tureen. She fancied the standard rose-trees which lined the path on either side were walking along with her; returning to the house she felt it was coming to meet her, and she was particularly pleased at the aspect of the lighted windows. The following morning, she would not be satisfied until she had been allowed to walk in the garden by daylight. Although she looked at everything with much interest, she was obviously not as pleased as on the previous evening.

The Danube flowing along the foot of the garden, she described as a long, broad, white band and pointed to where, in the landscape, the stretch of water began and ended. She imagined she could touch the trees in the Praterau on the farther side of stream. Since the day was bright, she was not able to bear the glare in the garden for long. She herself begged that her eyes might be bandaged again, because they ached and she felt a trifle giddy. When the bandage had been replaced, she was afraid to take a single step on her own account, although in the days of her sightlessness, she moved freely in places that were familiar to her.

With the recovery of this sense she became more distrait, and had to spend some time in thought before starting to play pieces on the piano which she had in former times performed with absolute precision at her recitals. Now that her eyes were opened, she found it very difficult to play anything at all. She sat observing her fingers as they scampered over the keys, but smudged most of the passages she played.

The report sounds extremely authentic, purposeful, yet intimate. It comes from an authentic source—her father's testimony which cannot be disputed by any agency, medical or scientific.

24

My Firm Belief

Faith can move mountains is an adage as old as the hills. It expresses a sublime belief, held by men of every known race and era that there is a force controlling all creation- a force which is all- knowing, supremely well-ordered, magnificent, purposeful and overwhelmingly just. To the primitive mind, even the everyday movements of nature, the physical manifestations of creation, were painfully incomprehensible and incoherent. Yet mankind realised, however dimly, the unseen, yet omnipresent something which controlled all life and all matter.

As mankind grew in number, there arose men and women of exceptional understanding, who seemed to appreciate and comprehend the inexhaustible riddle of creation. Their knowledge arose not from human memory or experience, but through an inner attainment with the unseen power behind everything. Many of these men were uneducated in the skills and knowledge of human nature but they seemed to be illuminated with an inner light, which bestowed on them not only great understanding, but also supreme confidence, contentment and often, a phenomenal control over the forces of nature.

All these men invariable spoke of a fountain of love, justice, compassion, a divine, omniscient being, which called creation into existence, to fulfil a purpose: the voluntary, self-propelled realisation of *oneness* with itself. Let us imagine this Divinity, as a supreme, exquisite, perfect form of Energy, which seeks to draw unto itself, more energy, by allowing a created matter to transform its substance from a base divinely perfect form till it can emerge with the "supreme power".

Seen this way, all creation, whether planets, stars, plants, animals or men are in various stages of realisation, of achievement of oneness with the Divine Eternity. Let us regard man as a high form of energy, well on the way and to its fulfillment endowed with the knowledge óf achieving divinity. The proof is there all around us, and has been ever since history was recorded, of men and women, who are called "enlightened beings" who were already one with Divinity. These human beings held aloft the light of knowledge, the wisdom which would enable all men and women to see the true path, the fulfillment of the motive of creation, their oneness with the eternal blissful poser. These men had powers which defied natural laws, because they derived they from the primal source of all creation itself.

I am a doctor — a healer of men's bodily afflictions. I am writing this book to share with you my experience of how attunement with the Divine Power can help you to lead a happier, healthier and more purposeful life. It is also my purpose to show you that the poser of our science is so very little when compared to the absolute scope of the Power that created the Universe. I am not a theologian or a philosopher. My interest is the healing of the bodies and minds of my fellow beings. I have been educated in the knowledge and skills of our science of healing. My purpose in writing this is to show you that the scientific men only treat but only HE cures.

If you are in tune with Divinity, you can achieve harmony of mind, body and soul, Sickness, diseases and unhappiness are alien to the human being. It is only when we are not in harmony with our creator that sickness comes. I wish to show to you how harmony can offer you access to powers which will not only help you to help yourself but to help others as well. I will show you what an immense storehouse of power the human mind is and what unimaginable feats it is capable of.

All of us have power. How to use this power purposefully is the question. Since my life is dedicated to healing the sick, I will show you how the human mind can and has, through harmony with our creator, effortlessly transcended seemingly iron formed laws of nature.

Let me place before you facts- fact which are beyond credence, which will explain to you that there is much more to this world than we have hitherto believed, and that divine assistance, the help of the Creator Himself is ours for the asking if only we would ourselves, as instruments, be worthy of divine grace.

The subject of this book is psychic or spiritual healing, which is the direct intercession of the Divine Will, or a good soul, through a human instrument or medium. Spiritual healers have cured cases of cancer, asthma, tuberculosis, arthritis, skin diseases, heart ailment ever mental and emotional disturbances.

Even the best healers cannot say what exact forces are at work or how the actual healing takes place. My endeavour in this book is to try and explain the fascinating, awe-inspiring complexity and duality of man and the universe, which is material and non-material, and the pioneering role of spiritual healers in the continuing voyage of discovery of ourselves and our world.

A prominent Soviet doctor who has done extensive research in parapsychology and Divine Healing has endorsed the work of a famous psychic healer with and open mind. In his published document in *Gulf News,* April 30, 1981 of the doctor writes:

> Mrs. Davitashvili, aged 36, can diagnose and treat illnesses by waving her hands along her patients, bodies. President Leonard Brezhnev, the Soviet leader and many other top Soviet official have been treated by this Psychic Healer.

Dr. Irina Checkmachev, chief doctor of the well-known state Planning Committee Clinic in Moscow has, according to the *Gulf News,* Said that Mrs. Dzhuna Davitashiviti made the same diagnosis as doctors in 97 per cent of the dozens of cases she studied there recently. The doctor revealed that in about half the cases, Mrs. Davitashvili also discovered additional maladies which the doctors confirmed subsequently by normal clinical methods. The Soviet newspaper *Pravda* has establishment of a special centre where " biofield" phenomena could be studied thoroughly. The paper further said that her patients included people "known to every one". Yet another research study published about the healer's work confirms that the healer is able to sense changes in the biofield that reveals psychological problems: "When I have my hands along the body of patient, I immediately can say what precise organs of his body are not functioning. Different illnesses evoke different feelings in my hands. There is no miracle here. Around every living organism including man, there is a biological field which we, extra-sensors, feel very well." These biofield changes depend on the physical and even psychological state of the organism, says Mrs. Davitashviti.

Dr. Giridhari Sharma, an eminent cardiovascular surgeon attached to Bombay Hospital for more than three decades, writes:

> You may have heard of Castellot, who had grown perfect silk worms from the eggs laid by a virgin, but this was disbelieved. Today this fact is not only accepted by naturalists and scientists, but is also universally accepted; though it was supposed to be contrary to one of widest and best established laws of nature, it is today admitted to be true and the supposed law, therefore, ceases to be universal. Similarly, reputed miracles in healing have been due to yet unknown laws of nature. We admit, we do not yet know what nerve of life-force really is or how it acts or can act and in what degree it is capable of transmission from one human being to another. It would be sheet ignorance on our part to affirm that under no exceptional conditions could phenomena, such as the cure of many diseases or perception through other channels than the ordinary senses, ever take place.

Scholars and students of different religions of the world and so also of psychic phenomena, know that the holy men in the far east, the saints of India and the lamas of Tibet who possessed the gift of healing and powers of precognition spent many years undergoing penances, self-sacrifices, meditation, fasting and special prayers. This was obviously done to achieve Spirit-power which is also called *Prana.* In monasteries and lamaseries these holy men have achieved supernormal powers which they used for the benefit of mankind and service of God. They stand as landmarks in the religious scriptures and are considered masters guiding us, particularly the healers, to serve humanity. They lived much longer, healing their lives and possessed not only healing posers but also other psychic abilities like intuitive diagnosis of diseases, materialisation and curing patients thousands of miles away through their healing intercession. In the twentieth century, the name of a Supreme Master who took Mahasamadhi in 1918 stands aloft. He is Sai Baba of Shirdi. A voluminous literature speaks of Sai Baba's supra-normal power, which he exercised for the welfare of humanity and yet lived the life of a fakir.

These holy men did not have any knowledge of human anatomy, much less any diseases. They were powerful instruments chosen by God to heal the sick.

Food for Thought

There can be no good health without proper nutrition and there can be no proper nutrition without proper assimilation of food. Thus, one of the first things psychic healing does is that it re-establishes normal conditions in this regard and builds up proper assimilation. In the stomach lies the first and last step towards recovery.

Imperfect nutrition causes the blood to become poor and weak and consequently, every cell in the body becomes starved. It is thus very necessary to take in proper amounts of water. Perfect secretion and excretion requires a lot of fluid intake, failing which, the secreting glands are unable to manufacture enough juices that aid digestion, absorption and assimilation. Even the excreting glands are restricted from throwing out waste from the kidneys and bowels. The liver is perhaps the worst affected organ.

25

The Etiology of Psychic Healing

Psychic healing can be broadly defined as healing energy channelled through a so-called world of spirits to cure human ailments. This channelling is done through the medium of human beings who allow their bodies to be used as the via-media to transfer such energy from one field to another.

This claim would immediately sound fantastic and outlandish. I am aware that some of you would be grinning, or grimacing. When I first heard it, i went through the same reaction. After all, even when the existence of a power called God is not yet scientifically proven, as we would say, without a shadow of doubt, how can one take for granted the existence of spirit? However "spirits" implies the existence of a disembodied energy-form after the physical death of person. Then again, this rests on the basis of an energy called "spirit" to be resident within humans during the course of his life and which gets liberated after his death.

I will not answer what would constitute the "proof" for a disembodied existence after death. I shall suggest reference to such famous scientists as Dr. George Meek of the United States, Dr. Friedrich Jurgenson of Sweden, Dr. Leslie Flint of the United Kingdom, Dr. Horoshi Motoyama of Japan and Dr. Franz Seidl of Austria. These scientists have done extensive research into this phenomenon and have come to the conclusion that some energy does exist after the physical death of a person. As there is no specific name allotted to this energy field, we shall call it "Spirits".

In fact, Dr. George Meek has published 12 significant reasons that empirically try to prove the existence of the spirit. As President of the Metascience Foundation in the USA, with branches in almost every country on earth, Dr. Meek has also been successful in canalising this energy through an electronic machine, which he calls Spiricom. The last product Spiricom IV has been able to interact, with another scientist, testified to be long dead.

Dr. Meek compares a human body to that of a caterpillar which is dead because his body is transformed into a butterfly and is, therefore, dead as a caterpillar. The butterfly, which symbolises the physically dead, admonishes the caterpillar in a verse from C. Eustance Owen's poem:

> Unhappy grub, be done with weeping,
> your sickly brother is not dead.
> He is stronger and no longer
> crawls like a worm, but flies instead.
> He dances through the sunny hours
> and drinks sweet nectar from the flowers.

Thus, at basic introduction of psychic healing, the existence of a post-physical energy is sought to be established. Also sought to be established are two other points: one that the post-physical living human through a sort of communication channel. And two, that both of these intelligence forms work together to alleviate a third person's suffering without primary resort to drugs.

26

Explanation of Psychic Healing Properties

The first property of psychic healing is that, it works. I say it through personal experience and have authenticated, certified and testified cases relating to over 47,009 ailing persons. In some cases, it has worked without any personal contact or touch with the patient concerned. Any of you is free to do further research on my patients if you wish, and my files are open to any unbiased, genuine researcher.

The second thing is that it works without a precondition of faith in the ailing person. Sceptics, atheists and unbelievers have been as equally cured as those with blind faith. As you would vouch, true science does not believe in faith, but proof. And what better proof can you get other than from a sceptical atheist with cancer who has tried every possible remedy without success and finally come to a psychic healer who gives him relief? Or what better proof can there be than a chronic migraine patient with intense pain finding that the pain has gone after a few visits to the specific psychic healer? Pain is a brutal, stark reality. And mere faith cannot wish it away.

The third point is that psychic healing does not necessarily require body-contact. Sending thought waves have also worked in psychic healing. Though there is not yet any scientific basis for telepathy, psychic healers all around the world have testified to the fact that just "praying", to use an unscientific word, works without touching the sufferer. As a corollary, therefore, distance does not count. The sufferer can be three miles away or 300,000 miles away from the healer. Thought transference in both cases is equal and real.

The fourth property is that psychic healing will *not* work unless compassion exists in the healer—compassion for the sufferer, empathy with his ailment, sympathy for this condition and a genuine desire to see that ailment disappears. Again there is no scientific recording of this compassion getting translated into energy fields. But I would suppose that compassion creates a state of attraction for the disembodied entity and makes it favourable for the entity to carry out its aim. According to me, compassion is the electrolyte, the human being is the catalyst and the cure is the creation between two elements: the entity and the sufferer. It thus represents a perfect chemical reaction.

The fifth property is that the therapy works within certain limit. Like all laws, psychic healing is not a certain unconditional cure. I shall classify broadly non-cures under the following headings:

1) Those that circumvent the law of nature, like amputated limbs, cut ears, noses, genetically blind, deaf or dumb persons and so on. No healing can regrow cut limbs or give sight to person without eyeballs or pupils etc.
2) Those that refuse to change their old environment. If a patient with tuberculosis stays in a colony where TB is rampant, no amount of healing will do anything for him.
3) Those that are genetically at fault. Dwarfs cannot be made to grow tall; genetically blind can not be given sight; low IQs cannot be increased and so on.
4) Certain cases with terminal illness in the in last stages. Cancer in the last stage cannot, normally, be cured, but the pain can be controlled. A person with a fatal heart attack cannot be prevented from it. And dead person cannot be brought back to life!

5) And finally, in certain unexplained cases. Some healers attribute these non-cures to so-called Karmic reasons, or the fruits of past actions, but scientifically speaking, I would just neglect this area as one which does not work for inexplicable reasons. But such cases are very rare indeed.

27

Forms of Psychic Healing

Broadly speaking, there are two forms of healing: *Contact Healing and Absent Healing.*

I feel, contact healing gives better results, but some healers find absent healing better and still some others think both work equally well.

On the other hand, psychic healing is universal and will work on all forms of life, including animals, birds, fish and so on, the only condition being that it should be willingly sought. Some healers show better results with animals. (To digress for a minute. If psychic healing rested on faith, how can animals, children and birds be cured by it? I do not believe animals can believe in this cure when even humans find it difficult to do so.)

The Historical Perspective

When people talk of history, one thinks of two or three thousand years ago. But I am not going to do that. Because that kind of time cannot be proved now. So I will refer to the last twenty years or so only.

I want to refer to three specific cases, of which one is still alive and can be physically examined if you wish. The three are Harry Edwards, Arigo and Tom Pilgrim.

I believe Harry Edwards was the greatest Psychic Healer of modern times. He healed 10,000 patients in just four years. According to his biographer, Ramus Branch: " To authenticate the cases, Edwards commissioned a team of chartered accountants and doctors to individually verify each case reported, check medical history in all cases and then certify the healing as being genuine." The 1954 Archbishop's Commission on Divine Healing condemned him, but later, was castigated by one of its own members who stated that they had misrepresented, distorted, ridiculed and then condemned an otherwise authentic healer.

Arigo of Brazil, whose real name was Jose P. Freitas used a rusty kitchen knife to heal a few hundred patients per day. Arigo was uneducated, carried out complex surgery using a small kitchen knife and could make complete medical diagnosis by merely looking at the patient. He was thoroughly "filmed" to rule out fraud.

Tom Pilgrim of England is still alive. His guide, or the disembodied entity, is Dr. Robert Koch (1843-1910), German bacteriologist and discoverer of the tuberculosis bacillus and winner of the Nobel Prize. Pilgrim is not a doctor but has testified to have done complete cures during trances, when his features begin to resemble those of Robert Koch. He practises out of Briton and is still considered as one of the leading psychic healers of the modern age.

To go into history for a second. The greatest healer or Psychic Surgeon was Jesus Christ. His laying on of hands is just what healers today do. In India, the Buddha was equally a great healer and so was Ramakrishna Paramahansa, the spiritual teacher of Swami Vivekananda. Another healer form India was the great Sai Baba, now revered as a Saint.

Applications of the Science

The foremost application is the alleviation of suffering. The primary suffering is of course pain, the next is the control of a disease and the third is the instilling of confidence and positive feelings.

If a patient with chronic illness finds his pain has gone, a major victory has been won. Pain is the window of a disease and if pain disappears, it is almost certain the disease will yield too. And once that happens, it is easier to instill confidence into the patients mind.

Psychic healing has been seen to work with viral illness, generic illness like deformed bones, tumours and so on and in certain congenital diseases like hormonal imbalances, organ malfunctions and so on. It also works well with atrophy and hypertrophy cases and in general those which do not come under clauses listed under "Explantation of Properties".

Food for Thought

Hippocrates, the father of medicine, wrote centuries ago: "The afflictions suffered by the body, the soul sees quite well with shut eyes". Wise physicians, even among the ancients, were aware how beneficial to the blood it was to make "slight frictions" with the hands over the body. Experienced doctors believe that the heat which oozes out of the hands when applicable to sudden and habitual pains and various forms of debility renovates and strengthens the body and the mind.

I have often experienced, while soothing my patients, as if there were a singular property in my hands, to pull and draw away from the affected parts aches and diverse impurities, by laying my hand upon the place and by extending my fingers towards it. It is thus known to some of the learned that health may be implanted in the sick by certain gestures, and by contact, as some diseases may be communicated from one to another.

28

The Mysterious Triad: Body, Mind and Soul

About two thousand years before the birth of Christ, Indian scholars writing in the Hindu holy scriptures, called the *Vedas*, stated: "The *Gayatri* is a prayer for the highest power that man is capable of possessing, called 'Dhi', or higher intelligence which brings him knowledge, mental and transcendental. What is eye to the body, Dhi, or intelligence is to the mind. This startling statement written so long ago, captures in one shot the essential link between the human mind and the soul or the psyche. It took Western philosophers 3,500 more years to come to a somewhat similar conclusion, when the founder of modern philosophy, Rene Descartes (1596-1650), declared his famous words, "Cagito Ergo Sum", or "I think, therefore, I am".

The very act of thinking, and therefore of being, enveloped the body and the mind. But Rene Descartes maintained that only humans could think, for they had "souls". He believed that knowledge by the sense is shared with animals, but animals have no soul. That is why they cannot think. The Roman Catholic Church then accepted this point of view.

Authentication about the existence of this third entity, the "soul", is available in the Christian *Holy Bible* as well. For proof, here are four paragraphs from Corinthians 15:42-45: "So too the resurrection from the dead. The body is sown in dissolution, it is raised in immortality. It is sown in dishonour; it is raised in glory. It is sown in sickness; it is raised in a spiritual body. There is a spiritual as well as a physical body. So it is written, 'The first man, Adam, became a living soul;' the last Adam became a life-giving Spirit."

Yet, our late twentieth century science has once again veered into two opposite camps over the entity called the "soul". One camp, composed of the so-called "Realists" and "Rationalists" and the "Existentialists", maintain that this non-mathematical variable called the "soul" cannot exist, for there is no positive proof of its being. The other camp, variously referred to as the "Fundamentalists" and "Dualists" and the "Believers" hold an exactly contrary view with somewhat the same reasoning that there is no positive proof that the "Soul does *not* exist; therefore, they maintain, it *does* exist. Both are valid in philosophy and perhaps, logic. And both could possibly be valid in science.

I would like to propound a different path. I am not a dogmatic follower of either camp. I belong to another category, called the "spiritualist" and I go by the assumption that the "soul" might exist, but from a rationalistic point view. According to me, is life itself. The spark that differentiates a living object from a dead or inanimate one, is the "soul". For more dramatic effect, consider a human being just on the verge of death. The moment death takes over, *something* obviously leaves the man, else, all bodily and mental functions would not stop so suddenly and irreversibly.

Thus, the "soul" according to me, encompasses the body and the mind or their great essences. It includes such variables as personality, behaviors, intelligences, genetic and environmental inheritances, quirks, defects and motivations.

Therefore the "soul", to put it in scientific terminology, is to very closely akin the "psyche", but is a little more than it. The "soul" is alive, because of its links with the body and the mind (whereas the "psyche" is not). The "soul" is emotionally inclined toward good or evil or its grades (while the "(psyche" is neutral); and the soul might live on after the death of the body that houses it, in the form of thought waves (ever as the "psyche" dies with the death of the human body).

Clinical and experimental psychology as well as modern psychiatry has for long concerned itself with just the "mind" and the "psyche" of the individual and ignored the correlation between the "body" and the "soul" which form the two other parts of a human being. (The great German psychologist, Sigmund Freud, first filled this gap by bringing in the body's unfulfilled urges, mainly sexual, in the understanding of the "psyche" and the "mind.") But few noted psychologists and philosophers have dared to publicly try to correlate the concept of "soul" in a deeper understanding to the body, mind and psyche.

That is the position I want to now urge upon you to consider. According to me, science need not isolate the so-called "soul" to try to study it. If it does, it would commit the same folly that medicine has been committing so long. I wish to state that a holistic consideration of the body, mind and psyche can answer most or all questions whose answers seem out of reach today. For, even mathematically, if one considers the "soul" as the essence of the human being, by studying the variable of that essence which are the body, the mind and the psyche, the answers to that essence or constant, could become clear.

A holistic outlook, according to me, is the best path toward getting answers to that essence or constant. A holistic outlook, according to me, is the path toward getting answers in medicine concerning the ills of the body and the mind—pathological, psychological and psychosomatic.

Arising out of these premises is the concept of the so-called "psychic" or "spiritual" healing, or the healing of the "soul" or the "psyche", so that it reflects that upon the physical body. I understand, most of us may look at such unorthodox and yet scientifically-being-researched therapies with some scepticism. However, I would like to point out the living testimony of the world's greatest modern healer, Harry Edward, who died in 1976 and put healing energy to test in the highly developed scientific world of Great Britain.

The miraculous healing posers of Harry Edward were thoroughly investigated by joint British medical teams (consisting of physicians, psychologists, radiologists, orthopaedists and others) as well as by the equally sceptical Anglican Church.

His spiritual healing sanctuary in Burrows (Lea, Shere, Guildford) in the UK, was visited by leading personalities doctors, journalists, movies as well as The European royalty. Almost 90 per cent of them (this figure could be an under-estimate) were miraculously cured by him when orthodox medical science had thrown in the towel. It even led the British Medical Council to accept "psychic" or "spiritual" healing as an alternative therapy.

Today, the healing work left over by Harry Edwards is surprisingly carried out in an equally amazing manner by Dr. B.P. Sahi and his colleagues in Patna. The Institute of healing and Alternative Therapy of India has been founded by Dr B.P. Sahi and their effective healing successes are as much known as those of Mr. Harry Edwards.

Unfortunately, psychic healing comes under the broad classification of ESP or Extra Sensory Perception, because a number of intuitive diagnoses is involved. But since this field is full of charlatans, tricksters and those out to make quick money the whole science had got bad name. So almost everybody dabbling in it gets labelled as a crook, which is unfair.

In the initial stages of surgery, barbers used to perform operations. Later, surgeons evolved. Just because some barbers continued to perform operations in the interim period, we did not label all surgeons as barbers, or vice versa. Similarly, ESP today is at a stage that surgery was some centuries ago. Some people are bound to take advantage of it. It would thus be more rational for men and women like us- doctors and scientists-to differentiate the so-called "ESP barbers" and the real "ESP surgeons", finish off the former and elevate the latter.

With the study of Psychic healing, and all other ESP activities, science can get a better insight into the "psyche" and the "soul." I would personally like scientists to dwell deeper this little-understood science. Man has just discovered that the atom is not the smallest particle in the world, that there are electrons, protons and neutrons and there are gluons, quarks and quasars, which are also energies. Maybe one day man may discover healing energy as the transfer of quasars, or even something with a lesser frequency.

But, as is normal, there is yet no available equipment to study these phenomena,. Can a camera ever capture a quasar? Can you quantify a radio signal that shoots into outer space? Similarly, right now, there is no machine yet available that can capture healing every on file or tape. And when we do not question the existence of quasars or radio waves or even gravity merely because we cannot quantify them, why should we question ESP, with so much in-build, prejudiced scepticism? I dare say, We should instead question the integrity of those who practise it and those who cheat hapless sufferers by false claims. But way also condemn those who are genuine, those who have objective, third-party proof of their efficacy?

This is circumstantial evidence, the best that science has so far. Psychic or spiritual healing energy takes the body as part of a holistic entity, including the mind, the psyche and the soul. That is one reason it is unorthodox, because we do not yet have a system of medicine that encompasses all these segments.

The reason allopathy has floundered with some of the most vicious diseases afflicting mankind is because of its refusal to consider the body as a part of the holistic triad. It is high time that the West had accepted the philosophies of the East and in fact, reexported them with additional vigour back to the East, which is rapidly and blindly accepting all the concepts put out by the West.

29

Hatred and Health

Physical science has for long taught that two opposing forces in nature cannot occupy the some slot of space. Thus gravity and anti-gravity, oxygen and hydrogen and matter and anti-matter cannot co-exist in the same frame.

But now, Newton's Third Law of Motion, that action and reaction are equal and opposite, is being applied with ease to biology and psychology. Worry and sound health cannot co-exist, feeling of threat cannot encompass love, and insecurity and sound digestion do not mix. What can, and does, co-exist is worry and ulcers, tragedy and cancers, tension and tachycardia and so on.

Science is veering around to took at disease of the mind. Never has the axiom, "a sound mind in a sound body" been more seriously taken by doctors than now. The first reaction of most top doctors today is to look for diseased body signals in the psyche. Emotional illness becomes suddenly more significant than physical ones.

The nervous system is to intertwined with the body and the mind that slight differences in one can immediately galvanise the other. Like a multimeter. A loss of position in office, the stomach goes wild; a threat to security, appetite dries up; loss of a loved one, the liver malfunction; fear of the unknown, the heart jumps all around; sudden stress on the job, the lungs go awry. The list is endless. And doctors don't know how to treat such cases.

The equal and opposite of courage is the "withdrawal" symptom. In the former, the body perks up to face up to the situation and in the latter, the body slackens down to take defeat and die. "It is all in the mind" is not just true today, but needs an additional clause, "And nowhere else". Condition your mind and the body can face any situation possible. Superman was never the body, it was the "Supermind" that controlled a normal body.

One way to dissolve tension and worry and all those negative feelings that engulf the mind is to blend with nature. Discovering the endless limits of ordinary, everyday nature around us—the birds, trees, animals, insects, earth—works magic on the mind and the body, just how or why that happens is a little down the road for science to discover yet.

Maybe a Fourth Law of Motions would be found and could pertain to-mental motion.

Lastly let us remember that to go against the evolution of things is to go against ourselves. This principle explains that upon foreseeing the end of a situation, the correct attitude is to accept it as completely as possible. Don't you agree that when you force something to an end, you produce the contrary." If you are moved by irrational impulses and force something against its own nature, you will see that though things may yield to your demands, sooner or later, they will return to oppose what you want to accomplish. Please realise that we are always living among apparent opposites which create contradiction and suffering for us. We must comprehend that these apparent opposites are different aspects of the same thing and could be used to our advantage.

30

The Right Attunement

Our ancient scriptures said it 2000 years ago and science is saying it now: our lives are motivated entirely by the thoughts we hold. But the question that science has not yet been able to satisfactorily answer is, where did the thoughts originally come from. The most logical answer is, from the brain.

But new research has shed more light on the brain itself. It is now perceived to be some kind of a biological, highly sophisticated radio receiver-an instrument that receives thought waves sifts these discards unwanted "interruptions" and "noise" and retains just what it was looking for.

Thoughts are more of things, of energy that is not yet measurable by crude scientific, high-precision instruments. They engulf the atmosphere like all other scientifically explained rays do, and human brains live off this vast reservoir of thoughts, like fish living off the ocean. It sustains them, feeds them, inspires them and gives them degrees of mental power.

Scientists are just finding out how thoughts govern lives. Surround yourself with beautiful objects and your distaste for the ugly grows more pronounced. Conversely, thing of hate, revenge, lust, greed and you attract just those "negatively charged thought-molecules" from the cosmos like a common magnet. Draw sustenance from great music, or a fine painting or good writing and you enable your mind and spirit to higher degrees. The body reacts just as quickly, following the thought pattern.

The ancients said the key to great living was nature. Modern science is just about saying the same thing. Mother nature is a repository of beauty, perfection, symmetry, class, art, music and originality. Tune in to nature and you are automatically attuning yourself to unadulterated peace and calm. Get outside of nature, and you block your reservoir like the fish blocking out water from its gills.

High thinking is the key to high living. Correspondingly, finding that right attunement is the key to right living. And it is modern science that is saying it, not some ancient traditional, iconoclastic ritual.

Most importantly and essentially, learn to like your own self unconditionally. Beware of self pity and come out of your shell in a positive way accepting the person you are. Avoid analysing everything others say or do. Learn to believe what you see and hear unless there is a genuine and evidential reason for doubt. Try hard and express yourself frankly to others. Show plenty of affection and speak out. Thus you must become involved. Relax all your defenses and become more and aware. Trust those who love you and expect trust and love in return. Practise noticing other people's feelings and responses. Use your imagination to its fullest and learn seriously what you are really capable of creating. Beware of your own behaviour and consider how it influences you and how you affect others.

Emotional states influence our entire nervous system. We feel our emotions in every part of our body. Mastery of emotional behaviour leads to control of much of our physical and psychological experiences. It is necessary to relax comfortably. Once you do this, it would be possible to practise imaging.

Remember any special occasion and place. There will be several such places worth remembering. Recall all of the sensations yourself while you were at that place. If you were at a hill station, remember the smell of clean air and the trees. Remember the stream. If you were at a beach hear the music of the waves and feel the warmth of the virgin sand. Then you choose more complex scenes on other days or occasions. Concentrate as effortlessly as possible on your old friends. Try and remember your host who called you for a dinner. Try and recall this vividly with all the people talking on different subjects. Feel purposely that you are there with those people "right now". Begin by seeing all the physical details of the situation. See the furnishings. Remember the paintings on the wall. See the view from the windows. Recall every detail. Try and be in that atmosphere physically and mentally, enjoying all the nostalgic events.

All this imaging will help you considerably in mental and physical relaxation, building up your nervous system and, of course, in simple but the right attunement.

31

Postface

The *Postface*, which include the concluding few lines of this book, deals with a galaxy of dignitaries from different walks of life who were and are presently treated with psychic healing, wholly or partially, either through contact healing (in person) or through absent healing (from a distance, in absentia).

I am afraid I cannot name them all. May be some of them may like to remain "unmentioned" for reasons best known tc them. May be some of them may sue me in a court of law because I do not have any evidence in support of the treatment they have received.

Twenty long years in healing have brought the so-called 'high' and the humble for their almost incurable ailments and yet, it is a pity that I am not supposed to mention some bit names! This anonymity means that I have not succeeded at all in curing two major diseases, namely EGO and the sense of Ingratitude. But it does not matter as long as I have succeeded in my mission to my entire satisfaction.

The names I can safely use, because I have the evidential proof to do so, are just a few as compared to an endless list of dignitaries in the Indian Film World, famous industrialists, doctors and surgeons, ministers and political party chiefs, media personalities, lawyers and barristers and very, important persons including the fabulously rich. They all came. They all were cured.

Despite limitations, I have on record names of people who mean a lot to me. Shri Shriyans Prasad Jain, the ex-chairman of Bombay Hospital, was perhaps the first person to be treated by me. It was a very lucky start. The next few in line were Shri Shantiprasad Jain and Shrimati Rama Jain, of The Times of India group of papers. Also, Shri C. Subramaniam, one of our most able ex-Finance Minister, and Shrimati Lalita Shashtri, the wife of our illustrious ex-Prime Minister. Then came Shri Ramakrishna Bajaj and Mr. M.V. Kamath, a brilliant author and columnist. Contacts became more rewarding as time passed. Loknayak Jayprakash Narayan was treated way back in 1975. Answers to my questions after his recovery, published in my book *Psychic Healing: My Personal Experiences* speak of the great man's sincerity in acknowledging publicly his views on phychic healing. The next patient to be "touched" was Swami Muktanandji of Ganeshpuri. Mr. Dilip Kumar Roy was the next luminary and his tribute to "My dear friend Dr. Keni" is also published in the book mentioned above. Then comes our ex-Prime Minister Shrimati Indira Gandhi, an equally cooperative and grateful patient.

One particular person stands out so prominently in my mind all these 14 years of close healing contact is Shrimati Amrita Pritam, an unforgettable personality, who has gone a step further in putting my work in one of her many books. A winner of the National Award for Literature and the Jnabpith and yet, so full of humility, which is a rare commodity in the present world. Then come three important personalities: Smt. Mrinalini Sarabhai, Smt. Tarkeshwari Sinha and Smt. Tara Ali Baig.

There are names and names but I must be careful in choosing them. Prof. Dr. Gunter Ammon, founder of German Academy for Psychoanalysis and the Dynamic Psychiatric Hospital Menterschweige, author of 400 scientific publications and more than 20 books translated into several languages, called me to Berlin and made it possible for me to do mass healing on hundreds of patients in the Berlin Hall and thereafter in the World Congress Meet in 1986. Dr. Lilia Logette also did the same for me in Florida. She is the Managing Director of the Psychical Research

Society of Florida—a landmark in the history of psychic science. Next to follow are Smt. Asha Bhonsle, whose name is legendary, and so are Smt. Kishori Amonkar, Pandit Shiv Kumar Sharma, Ustad Amjad Ali Khan and Smt. Sushma Kiran Kumar —a classical psychic and a wonderful human being, so rare to be found. Equally brilliant, is Mr. Raju Chellam, a versatile author of international repute. His association with me as a patient 20 years ago and as a close friend thereafter, is deeply cherished by me.

The list, as I have said, is endless, and therefore, I look forward to continue it, hopefully, in my next book.